SOCIOLOGY
Today

CHRISTINE L. MCCLURE

Kendall Hunt
publishing company

Cover image © Shutterstock, Inc.

www.kendallhunt.com
Send all inquiries to:
4050 Westmark Drive
Dubuque, IA 52004-1840

Printed in the United States of America
10 9 8 7 6 5 4 3 2 1

contents

CHAPTER *one*

THE BEGINNING OF SYSTEMATIC OBSERVATION

© Regissercom, 2012. Under license from Shutterstock, Inc.

EARLY SOCIOLOGISTS, ACTIVISTS FOR SOCIAL CHANGE, AND THEORETICAL PARADIGMS

This chapter will include the introduction to the scientific study of society from early European society to American social science research. Why do we need sociology in our lives today? Define the three sociological theories of functionalism, conflict, and symbolic interaction. Theorists, sociologists, and social activists include Auguste Comte, Emile Durkheim, Karl Marx, W.E. DuBois, Harriett Martineau, and Mary Jones (Mother Jones).

In the new millennium we are in a society transformed from years past. Myths and traditions have been accepted and rejected since early American history. Societies have inspired evolutionary thought through new inventions we never dreamed of including electricity, steam engines, computers, and genetic developments. Look up in the sky on any day and there we are in flight traveling thousands of miles to another country. Amazing! Each time I board an airplane and travel abroad or across the country I am astounded by the precise invention of the modern jet. Travel began in America with ships full of people enduring the arduous path across the Atlantic from Europe. Many people did not make it during the trip. Today this is rarely the case.

society
functioning
conflict
labeling
equality
structure

society

Understanding the dynamics of American history we see an American **society functioning** well, monitoring **conflict** through laws and policies, and **labeling** the norms of a new country based on freedom and **equality** for all. A **structure** in European society led to a new formation of democracy in early America up to the present. The change did not happen overnight. Hard work had to be done to be a society in transition.

norms
values
attitudes
sociology
sociologists

society

The scientific process of observing **norms**, **values**, and **attitudes** of the people in a specific land area is the field of **sociology**. Researchers who specialize in this field are called **sociologists**. A sociologist uses a scientific method—used in most fields in social sciences, humanities, medicine, and law—to analyze a society, a group of people who achieve traditions, norms, values, and attitudes and have a mutual concern for the people as a whole. Sociologists elaborate and measure the particulars of each society and make comparisons. By viewing one's own society we can analyze other societies with possibly the same or different attitudes

attitudes
beliefs

and **beliefs**. What can we learn from having a discipline such as sociology? We can learn how a society organizes, competes, and identifies the people who make it up. Does society create the individual or do individuals create society? What works for one society may not work for another society. What is a conflict or deviant to one society may not be for another society. What is symbolic and of value to one society, of course, may not be for another. So what can we learn from analyzing and comparing societies? These are all of the questions a sociologist presents to comprehend the field of sociology.

AUGUSTE COMTE

Auguste Comte (1798–1857) wrote the book, *A General View of Positivism.* Comte (1957) expresses the idea of positivism and polity which is the object of philosophy to present a systematic view of human life, as a basis for modifying its imperfections (p. 8). Comte is considered the "father of sociology" in many introductions to sociology textbooks. In contrast, he may be considered the "grandfather" of sociology

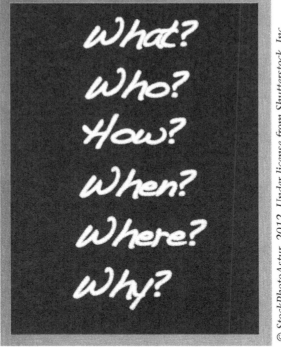

© StockPhotoAstur, 2012. Under license from Shutterstock, Inc.

as Herbert Spencer (survival of the fittest) who developed Comte's ideas, is recognized as the "first father" of sociology (Comte, 1957). Sociology is an unbiased approach to understanding society today. The proposed scientific method that Comte presented years ago describes science as a system of **objectivity** and process.

objectivity

Comte (1957) noted "the primary object, then, of positivism is two-fold: to generalize our scientific conceptions and to systematize the art of social life" (p. 3). In order to generalize, a method is needed that is accepted among those who study social life. **Social life** here can be noted as being the components of society as a whole. Specifically this would include every person, every institution, and every issue common to most in society. During this time, Comte designed a philosophical thought that was before the thought of society today. Social life was extremely different in the late eighteenth and nineteenth centuries. Looking at society over decades and centuries is an essential part of being a sociologist—that is, having the ability to view the past, the present, and make predictions into the future. Comte did just that.

social life

To be a sociologist today is no different. The society at large can be compared to society in France during the time when Comte lived. The two periods of time expose the individuals of society to a specific **environment** with similarities and differences. A sociologist will study how a society works, how it deals with disasters and conflict, and how people in each society **symbolize** the world in which they live.

EMILE DURKHEIM

Emile Durkheim (1858–1917) contributed and understood the systematic process that Comte set forth in positivism (Giddens, 1986). Durkheim, like Comte, was native to France. Durkheim wrote about suicide rates in Europe, religion, and how society structures itself. By providing a structure at the **macro-sociological** level, sociology can generalize to the rest of the population. Simply stated, we can look at the "big picture" and the direct and indirect influences society has on an individual and how an individual contributes to society.

Durkeim lived in the same country as Comte, but in a later period of time. Durkheim notes in his essay, *The Concept of the State,* about his society of France during his lifetime:

> "France is not only a mass of people consisting in the main of individuals speaking a certain language and who observe certain laws and so on, but essentially a certain defined part of Europe" (Durkeim, as cited in Giddens, 1986, p. 33).

Durkheim goes even further to establish the importance of a society and its relation to the collective people. "The society of which we are members is in our minds all the more a well-defined territory, since it is no longer in its essence a religion, a corpus of traditions peculiar to it or the cult of a particular dynasty" (Durkheim, as cited in Giddens, 1986, pp. 33–34). A *society* is defined as the collective whole of people who live in the same geographical location and are governed by the same state. Through state governance, individuals of society adhere to the ways of the society. Right and wrong become evident based on the laws of society creating the functionality of the system. If we know what is right in society we will know what is wrong, thus establishing the **morals** of society.

KARL MARX

Karl Marx (1818–1883), from Germany, is considered a **conflict** theorist defining the split in social classes based on the **division of labor**. Marx emphasizes "the division of labor presents just the first example of the fact that so long therefore as the split exists between the individual and the common interest, so long as activities are not divided voluntarily but by a process of natural growth, man's own act becomes to him an alien power standing over against him, dominating him, instead of being ruled by him" (p. 1). Marx was expressing the idea of **capitalism** and the structure of **social inequality** it creates. Sociologists also add where capitalism will take social inequality.

conflict
division of labor

capitalism
social inequality

Marx went on to state that unlike the capitalist society, "in a Communist society, each one does not have a circumscribed sphere of activity but can train himself in any branch he chooses, society by regulating the common production makes it possible for me to do this today and that tomorrow, to hunt in the morning, to fish in the afternoon, to carry on cattle-breeding in the evening, also to criticize the food—just as I please—without becoming either hunter, fisherman, or shepherd or critic" (p. 1). Here Marx is explaining the "right to live one's life the way one wants to" instead of being controlled by our bosses—a true aspect of a capitalist society. What would Marx think of the extent of capitalism today?

Marx continued on to reveal "in all history up to now it is certainly an empiric fact that single individuals, with the expansion of their activity to a world historic scale, have become more and more enslaved to an alien power....a power which has become steadily more massive, and has turned out to be, in the last analysis, the *world market* " (pp. 1–2). Marx clearly mentions the idea of the global market and the surge of global capitalism. His concern here is what is going to happen to most people in society based on a capitalist structure. In a capitalist structure we will see less quality of life and a complete adherence to the enslavement of the corporation. Power and control is created and abused. Workers are exploited, as capitalists get richer. Karl Marx clearly was concerned that the labor schedule and market would leave little rights left for workers—a practical slavery.

W.E. DUBOIS

A prominent sociologist, W.E. DuBois (1868–1963) was a leader and social science researcher in the field of African-American studies. DuBois was born on the day after the birth of George Washington was celebrated in the city of Great Barrington, which lay between these mountains in Berkshire County in western Massachusetts (DuBois, 1968, p. 61). He states in one of his later biographies: "...the year of my birth was the year that the freedman of the South were enfranchised, and the first time as a mass took part in government" (DuBois). Conventions with the black delegates voted new constitutions all over the South and two groups of laborers—freed slaves and poor whites—dominated the former slave states (DuBois). The era DuBois grew up in could have been his major influence toward a "striving equal society." Unfortunately, DuBois had many obstacles to overcome. Freed slaves and poor whites of the nineteenth century were in a social class destined by capitalists—that is, mostly rich white Europeans in early America—to remain oppressed in the lower class.

social class disparity
sociologist
racism
social class oppression

DuBois observed a **social class disparity**, an important aspect of being a sociologist then and today, amongst the colored. Is color the basis for **racism** here or is **social class oppression** of the colored the basis for racism? This period in American history provides explanation to the **social construction of racism** (as we will discuss further in Chapter 9). DuBois saw little and knew less about his father. His mother reared him and emphasized the importance of education and hard work. She taught him that anything is possible. DuBois's early years of education landed him educational opportunities at Harvard and in Europe. His writings told of the patterns and beliefs of a society not only in the United States, but also in nineteenth-century Europe. DuBois explains crisply: "...above all, science was becoming a religion; psychology was reducing metaphysics to experiment and sociology of human action was planned" (DuBois, 1968, p. 155). He notes additionally that "everywhere men sought wealth and especially here in America there was extravagant living among the rich and the rich planned to be richer; everywhere wider, bigger, higher, better things were set down inevitably" (DuBois). Here we see the expansion of **global capitalism** crossing advanced societies such as the United States and Europe.

As I conclude thoughts and insights on DuBois's philosophy and thoughts on racial relations, keep in mind DuBois grew up not being a slave, unlike his early generations. However, when exposed to the world, he saw the serious issues the United States and Europeans had with colored people. He spent many years of academic and methodological research dedicated to bettering the attitudes of our society so that "colored people" meant more than being poor, a slave, and uneducated. His work is vastly important for people of all colors in a world where oppression and slavery of people is used for profit and the benefit of those with power and wealth. DuBois's writings bring the nineteenth century thought to today. Are we still practicing the abovementioned activities? Sociologists observe the bigger picture—that which is happening to all people of a society. Our society is part of a macro-sociological understanding of the world as a whole. We will continue to explore our role in this world.

HARRIET MARTINEAU

As DuBois talked of the American pursuit of profit, so did Harriet Martineau (1802–1876). She traveled far and wide, and observed

social construction of racism
race
ethnicity

global capitalism

macro-sociological role

the politics of the economy. Martineau (1837[1966]), an English scholar, describes nineteenth-century U.S. politics:

> It seems strange that while politics are unquestionably a branch of moral science, bearing no other relation than to the duty and happiness of man, the great principles of his nature should have been neglected by politicians—with the exception of his love of power and desire of gain—till a set of men assembled in the State House at Philadelphia, in the eighteenth century, and there throned a legitimate political philosophy in the place of a deposed king (pp. 3–4).

Martineau observed as an early sociologist the need to keep morals intact with politics—a dire task that today has crossed immoral boundaries. Maybe we can use Martineau's work and theory to gain back morality in our political system, helping society by helping all people in the United States of America. What do you think? Are we that far off from basic morality that we cannot bring the political economy back to **homeostasis**—balancing morals, **politics**, and **economy** with a humane approach protecting all and striving for a country that loves its people and shows it through its economic and political systems?

homeostasis
morals
politics
economy

Martineau was a European traveler and observer to the United States in the nineteenth century. "The traveler from the Old World

© kentoh, 2012. Under license from Shutterstock, Inc.

to the New is apt to lose himself in reflection when he should be observing" (Martineau, 1837[1966], p. 208). Harriet Martineau is doing sociology work here. She compares herself to the norms of people in a society. As a sociologist she is analyzing far more than most in a **methodological process**. Sociologists like Martineau want to piece together each part of society as a whole. In sociology we do not want to leave out a portion of society that may supply why something happens or why it does not.

KEY TERMS

methodological process

MARY HARRIS (MOTHER JONES)

As a very modern-day sociologist, I am inclined here to add, for the first time in any sociology textbook, the less-talked-about social activist/sociologist during the nineteenth century, Mother Jones (Mary Harris). I took four years of American and world history in high school in the late 1970s and early 1980s, never learning an "ounce" about Mother Jones. I was born an American in the late 1960s, living here my entire life never hearing or knowing about Mother Jones. She is a true American social hero, activist, and yes, sociologist. She understood her society—how it functions, how it is a conflict, and what it really means to American people. She grasped and inhaled the plight of coal miner families and workers in the nineteenth century. I am stumped as to why her life was not an important part of my educational years. I can remember asking my American history instructor in high school if there was a woman who made contributions to history. He replied, "No." So I am writing this to introduce to you someone who has been underreported, underrated, and underexplored in the field of sociology.

Mary Harris (her real name) was married to a coal miner and had four children. She encountered the poverty, demise, and exploitation of workers in the nineteenth century who worked in the coal mines for those who owned it. Harris watched helplessly as her husband and children died from a plaque At the age of 60, she began traveling around the country after she observed the exploitation of workers. As a sociologist myself, I am also concerned about the plight of immigrants (legal and illegal), impoverished working conditions for the lower- and middle-class workers, and solidarity for workers in a free country like the United States of America.

Harris began her activism without fear, but inspirable fervor, for typical Americans of the time. She went above and beyond what most Americans deem necessary, giving to others and organizing workers to take charge of being in a "free" country that represents due process. Harris became known as Mother Jones to the workers of this country as she helped those who were less fortunate. She was a sociologist in every right—examining, refuting, and observing the society around her. Mother Jones made social change forces for early Americans so they could have rights as workers. Her activism brought a voice to thousands of people being exploited by labor.

CHAPTER ONE *summary*

Sociologists in history studied society and observed patterns of group behavior. Auguste Comte, the founder of sociology, created a lens to see the order, conflict, and labels of the collective whole. Comte reflected the turmoil in France during a chaotic era. The idea that society maintained harmony despite the conflict poses a discussion in sociological thought. If we understand what works in society, as Comte saw, then we can explain the discourse. The social order permeates society. The social conflict also remains. Together society balances order and conflict.

Emile Durkheim added to Comte's work in sociology by emphasizing structural functionalism. The public at large creates roles essential for society to complete tasks, goals, and necessary functions to be efficient. Durkheim studied rates of suicide in Europe resulting in an understanding of the importance of social integration of humans. The more one isolates oneself, the more likely a sense of anomie (normlessness) progresses. Durkheim greatly advanced the field of sociology by understanding groups of people as a whole. If a person does not have a group to which to belong and work, then seclusion sets in. According to Durkheim we need to be with other people in order to function as humans.

Karl Marx had his eye on people in society as Durkheim did. Marx, however, could not see the necessity of working for others and being enslaved to the bourgeoisie. Working exploited the lower class, noted Marx. People did it not to help society and themselves function but to help the capitalists get richer. Marx did not like the idea of being on the time clock as we do in our society today. He felt that the common people are losing themselves when working as what he called the proletariat. Marx knew that profit came at an expense to the commoners. Marx was the prominent conflict theorist in sociology.

Another conflict theorist in sociology is W.E. DuBois. He was the first African-American sociologist. DuBois was born and raised in western Massachusetts. He received an education despite the fact that many of his family before him were enslaved in early America. He did not notice the racial tensions in American society until he grew up. He made race relations his life research and passion after being exposed to the extreme segregation in his adult years. Being the only African-American studying at Harvard, DuBois experienced segregation firsthand. His research was geared toward making opportunities for African-Americans who were severely impoverished and disadvantaged even after emancipation. His work is pivotal to creating a more equal society in America.

Female sociologist Harriet Martineau observed the connection between morality and politics. She saw the European culture of politics together with morality. In the United States this was not true. People are not being considered as a whole in American society. Politicians make way for one's own gain and less to the benefit of the people as a whole. Martineau had access to travel to compare and contrast societies politically and economically. She embraced the specified division of labor increase that happened during the birth of the agricultural and industrial revolutions.

Like Martineau, Mary Harris (Mother Jones) gave us so much in her later years of life. From the age of 60 to 90, she traveled the United States, helping to improve the rights of families who worked in the coal mines. She wanted the best for families in early America. She was amazing in every aspect of leadership for the common people who worked the menial or most dangerous jobs. Mother Jones died aspiring better conditions for lower-class workers and their families.

Sociologists like those mentioned in this chapter by far have seen society and detected the differences needed to create an American society that is equal, not exploited. I am sure if they were here today they would see better living and medicine, but the extreme exploitation of workers moves on.

Please answer the following discussion questions:

1. In your own life what do you observe about the society in which you live? What works well? What does not work well (i.e., is in a conflict)? Provide specific examples from the book and from your own life.
2. Pick a sociologist of interest from this chapter. Write a one- to two-page paper researching their background and contributions to society. Why are you interested in this sociologist? Please explain.
3. Why do you think sociology is important to discuss and to understand in history, both now and in the future?

SOCIOLOGICAL KEY TERMS

1. Society
2. Functioning
3. Conflict
4. Labeling
5. Equality
6. Structure
7. Norms
8. Values
9. Attitudes
10. Sociology
11. Sociologist
12. Beliefs
13. Objectivity
14. Social life
15. Environment
16. Symbolize
17. Macro-sociology
18. Morals
19. Conflict
20. Division of labor
21. Capitalism
22. Social inequality
23. Social class disparity
24. Racism
25. Social class oppression
26. Social construction of racism
27. Global capitalism
28. Homeostasis
29. Politics
30. Economy
31. Methodological process

CHAPTER *two*

THE TEN SOCIAL INSTITUTIONS TODAY

© Eddie Pell, 2012. Under license from Shutterstock, Inc.

APPLICATION OF FUNCTIONALISM, CONFLICT, AND SYMBOLIC INTERACTION

This chapter will elaborate on how the three sociological theories—functionalism, conflict, and symbolic interaction—can be applied to each of the ten social institutions providing an objective approach to understanding society today. Education, the family, religion, health care and medicine, military, media, politics, economy, law, and science can be functional, a conflict, and symbolic to our society today. This chapter will provide this in detail.

In the preceding chapter we examined sociologists and their thoughts. Sociologists offer a viewpoint on society that is objective. Sociology is similar to looking outside of what we recognize. Just when we assume we comprehend society, we don't. How exciting is that?! Knowledge in the academic field of sociology is based on a continuum. In the United States, the approach we envision to studying social institutions is diverse and at the same time parallels our view of life in U.S. society. In this section we will survey everyone's observations. Civilization changes while perceptions assimilate and adjust. The splendor of the three sociological theories is, no one human being is right and no one individual is wrong. It exists, as it combines ideas from the community of social order.

FUNCTIONALISM

society

In the first chapter we discussed the subject matter of Emile Durkheim and Auguste Comte. Both are considered historically functional theorists in sociology. This is the idea that **society** holds a foundation providing order and structure. Without order and structure in society it would be difficult to be efficient, especially with large numbers of people living in a culture, as is the case in the United States today. According to the 2012 U.S. census, there are an estimated 313 billion people living here, and the following incidences are happening in the time clock as of March 12, 2012:

1. One birth every 8 seconds
2. One death every 12 seconds
3. One international (net) migrant every 46 seconds
4. Net gain of one person every 15 seconds

population growth

Population growth is constantly on the increase both here and around the world. Longevity has increased due to quality of life, and improved medicine and health care. We can live longer than humans did hundreds of years ago.

How can we function with a population so large? The structures at the federal, state, and county levels are described as overworked and understaffed. If the population grows, then so does the need for better standards in social institutions. Programs at the federal and state levels include Social Security, Medicare, and Medicaid. When these programs began, the demographics were vastly different. Today the programs are being fine-tuned and organized to make our system work. How can we improve upon the dynamic system efforts? What may be functional to one person may not be for others. Whoever is in power to make a system will enhance the ability to say what is functional and what is not. To work and to provide order sustains a functional society.

CONFLICT

In stark contrast the systems of the United States may appear not to work. The conflict perspective, expressed diligently by Karl Marx, sends a message that social institutions and networks may not be working efficiently. For example, those who work for others have less **power and control** over their lives and labor. **Competition** is evident due to the lack of resources. Individuals see social institutions serving the few, not the majority. He warned workers there would be a loss of freedom in a capitalist society. Many would agree with Marx today, although many may not, because this is the opinion of one person. But what is the collective whole saying regarding the competition over scarce resources, and power and control issues? We will apply functionalism and conflict to broaden the perspective of social institutions and social issues.

SYMBOLIC INTERACTION

As we look at applying functionalism and conflict theories to social institutions we need to heighten awareness of social institutions with the symbolic interaction theory. This micro-sociological theory envisions one-on-one social interaction. The use of language and symbols compose this theory of social interaction. People in society use language to communicate and stereotype life and scenarios. Labeling is natural for people. We learn at a very early age to put words to meaning. Society depends on this to be effective. Where would we be if we did not stereotype? Human beings are unique. We use words to identify

power and control
competition

family members, streets we travel on, food we eat, and the colors we see (just to name a few).

APPLICATION OF THE THREE SOCIOLOGICAL THEORIES TO THE TEN SOCIAL INSTITUTIONS

Education

Functionalism

The social institution of education is vital to people and communities. Let's explore how education is functional, a conflict, and symbolic in America today. Education is functional in several ways; however, many will not find the same reasoning or subjective approach as to why education is functional in society. We know that children in the United States have to go to school from kindergarten through the twelfth grade. College is not mandatory in this country, but it is a **value** for numerous Americans.

Education is functional as it provides knowledge, skills, and the criteria to achieve new skills considered necessary to promote one's aspirations and careers. Schooling employs teachers, staff, and administration, allowing the opportunity to make money to care for oneself and others. Education brings awareness to people about social problems and questions what appears to be true. Children learn discipline, values, and group dynamics that will help them in the real world. Education entitles each child to a socialization process (developmental sociology), creating for all students ways of coping and becoming resilient. Social interaction is significant to being human. The institution of education allows this environment optimally. Learning is functional to all of us from the time we are born to the time we die. Education can be necessary for humans to grow physically, socially, and emotionally.

Conflict

Education can also be a conflict noting the competition to do better than others and maintaining a highly "competitive edge." Students work hard in the United States, juggling employment, family and other relationships, and college studies. A person trying to manage so many responsibilities discovers less time for

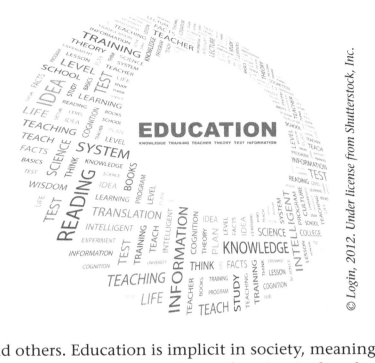

© Login, 2012. Under license from Shutterstock, Inc.

self and others. Education is implicit in society, meaning we take it for granted that it has to be done. Education is also a business in the **global market of capitalism** and the **pursuit of profit**. In various countries education is free. Here in the United States the cost of education is high and continues to rise.

global market of capitalism
pursuit of profit

I was in Chicago attending the National Education Conference this year. Students were picketing there against the rise of tuitions and student debt. The students marched in front of the university in downtown Chicago demanding lower costs in education. Many students know they may go to their graves paying off student loans in order to live the American dream of a higher education. Education is a conflict as the people who have more money have better quality education, access to the best private schools and colleges, and preparation for important tests such as the ACT, SAT, and for graduate school the GRE and the GMAT. If we are to measure one's ability to finish a high school education by one bias and specific examination are we really a society creating education for all?

Another aspect of the conflict theory for the social institution of education is the amount a teacher is paid for teaching in comparison to other occupations. In higher education there are more part-time than full-time instructors. The part-time instructors have little job security and benefits like health care, office space and computers, and seniority. K-12 instructors, preschool, and day care workers are paid minimal wages compared to the years of education put into the career. Conflict in education comes with consequences here in the United States. The **social class disparities** remain evident. This is a serious abuse of the system in a country where equality is pivotal to the values of an **American culture**.

Symbolic Interaction

Symbolically, the mention of American education does persuade American culture. When we label American education today there is the **ideology** that the wealthy have the means to get an education. We view education as a "**way to the American dream**," but when we stereotype American culture specific to the social institution of education, undoubtedly American students in colleges will exclaim, "I have to get an education. It is the only way to get ahead." However, the reality is most students will owe more than they could ever imagine owing to get that American dream. So the stereotype and label, as projected for the theory of symbolic interaction is education costs money, but it's worth it to spend thousands of dollars to get there. Education is symbolic to Americans as it represents the ability to build credentials to obtain work. Education represents an American way of life that is expected of us from the day we are born.

Family

Functionalism

Next is the social institution of the family, the most precious unit we have in U.S. society. The family unit brings money to businesses, including education, media and television, and the profitable companies such as "Babies-r-us, Disney World, Universal Studios, and Wal-mart." Where would these companies be economically without the social institution of the family? Functionalist theory allows us to explore how the family, social institutions, and social issues work for us—for most of us, that is. Family is dynamic to our society. If we look at the numerous families in the United States we can see them as consumers contributing to the success of a business or society in general.

We continue to analyze the **provided function** of the American family today. Are families teaching children values

© wavebreakmedia, 2012. Under license from Shutterstock, Inc.

or contributing more to the economics of our society? Sociologists have studied the institution of the family beginning in the 1970s. Dr. Murray Straus, professor emeritus in sociology, from the University of New Hampshire has conducted research on the family here and abroad. Straus (2008) has transformed the function of families in society to more than raising children and feeding them, but to treating American children and parents with respect in discipline, positive social interaction, and the importance of having an unconditional mentor/parent/ guardian.

I can remember growing up in the 1960s and 1970s in a lower- to middle-class family of five. My family, like many families, cherished less from children in demands of communication, but more in labor (i.e., "Children were to be seen, not heard."). The ideology of the families since that time has changed. The generation one grows up in is what we expect and what we know. As we become parents society will change. We no longer discipline children the same way since new research and times have transformed. I will not expect my children to have a family the same as mine (as will most families in the United States). It is just simply unrealistic.

Modern families are functional to our society. The main function of a **modern family** is to nurture family members unconditionally, support each other, reproduce or adopt, provide economic stability, teach values of society (this means legal activities), seek out resources when in need of help, and cope in a positive manner. These are the critical aspects of a modern family. As a family researcher specializing in domestic violence across the

modern family

lifespan, I have seen and read what can go wrong with a family. We need to make the family a priority in American society today and in the world. This is another major function of the family in society, to be the most important social institution. With that being said, families are significantly functional in our society. Families bring society the necessities of being human. Families care, support, and need reciprocity from business, government, and communities to make each other stronger. That is the function of the family today, not to be less of a commodity or to be exploited in labor. Families every day on a continuum have the MOST important role of all institutions, to care for the young, the old, and for the well-being of society.

Conflict

The family as a social institution can be a conflict competing over scarce resources and dealing with power and control issues. In a family the last thing that is supposed to happen is power issues—the control of one over another. In this century, we know what is healthy in a modern family and what is not. Incest is illegal and abusive. Abuse is illegal and abusive. In our day and time, control over an individual is not acceptable. Child sexual abuse, incest, and spousal abuse is a conflict—a major conflict. People are not to be treated this way.

When in history has that standard been met? Well, we can certainly understand that in American society this is not only illegal, but mandatory. Abuse is a conflict in families today. Who has the right to control other people? This is not only outdated, but not the way we treat individuals in our society today. Let's make it a wrong as a norm and a fad of the past.

Sibling rivalry has been obviously around for years, but it is a conflict. What role does a parent and society play in the modern family? A child can be exploited, abused, and the least recognized emotionally exploited and abused. Emotional abuse is the last resort in our society to have control over an individual. It is a key sign or flag to even more severe abuse. We do not discuss emotional abuse today in our society. We may scope the idea of "bullies" in school, but neglect family members who are abusing loved ones emotionally in their homes. It is time to recognize the psychological abuse of individuals in relationships and in families. There is no law to stop or recognize this long-lasting and damaging abuse to family members. Projecting one's dominance to the point of abuse is unlawful. Nevertheless, we are still in need of laws to protect American citizens from the torment, manipulation, and devastating consequences of emotional abuse.

Symbolic Interaction

The family is less respected symbolically in the United States today. We do not put an important emphasis on the family; this is the ideology of the country. When we label the family in the present day it is without doubt costly, intricate, and one of many roles or chores an American must face in the new millennium. As a family researcher, I hear the importance of one's own family. However, I do not see the priorities essential for families to survive. This is no fault of the family unit, but of a society that emphasizes the substance of wealth as the central lesson.

The family can be rich, poor, maybe somewhere in between, functional, dysfunctional, and/or vibrant or miserable. The family can be drained by one or two members who choose to make irrational decisions that can affect them for a lifetime. Can you imagine being a son or daughter of a serial killer, rapist, or a corporate giant who stole millions from individual retirements? The label we would apply to the family relations still pervades the lives of the innocent left behind. It's a tough society for children and families today, and even more so when family members do not pull their weight.

Overall, the family can be measured or labeled their weakest link. The example would be a scale of how effective a family can grow in times of crisis presented to them. Keep in mind the assessment is a tool not to judge a family, but to bring awareness to how much more the family can be at the optimal level. Many families and individual members tend to be quite unaware of their surroundings. At the symbolic level this presents the family as working well in society (when in fact this may not be the case). A family works well only at the level it sees itself. With this scale there can be more awareness that development and growth of the family unit can be done. I would like to further mention it is imperative that the other family members not consider themselves or others as "bad." The scale is there to bring awareness to those who choose to recognize the reality of the situation.

Religion

Functionalism

modern religion

Religion is such a vast word in the United States today. What does religion mean in the year 2012? Religion is defined in a modern view. **Modern religion** is spirituality, dedication to one philosophy or thought, inspired by arts and nature, meditative and reflective, optimistic, altruistic, and inspirational. Religion is different for our society compared to other societies. What works for one society or person with respect to religion requires a different opinion or meaning for another. **Ideology** is part of religion as much as values. We perceive countless Americans with a straight move toward what may or may not be the same as their family or even their best friend. This is a crucial feature of belief in American society today.

ideology

Religion in America critically means choice. We wake up every day finding our beliefs, values, and attitudes representing a modern religious or value system. I am noting here that religion and values are the same for contemporary society. What we expose to others and to close family members emulates our value system. Many Americans believe religion is functional in society since we have the ability to choose our religion and value system, which varies from the traditional view, when religion provided the laws, morals, and values of society. What is true and functional about religion in our society in the present is that it brings us comfort and flexibility along with the ability to choose the value important to each of us. **Traditions** and **rituals** are very functional in American culture. Weddings, funerals, baby showers, and birthdays remain pervasive. Holidays such as Christmas, Easter, and St. Patrick's Day reflect the functional aspect of our value system in America. Many of us may celebrate Christmas and Easter, yet in a traditional American way and in a less religious manner.

traditions
rituals

Conflict

Freedom of religion is a fundamental right in the United States. If someone or some group tries to push their ideals on you or others it then becomes a conflict. Values sometimes do not synergize. People and countries have killed in order to conquer others' values and beliefs. In a contemporary society there is still oppression of people based on religious freedom and values of society. One should have a choice to pick one's own religion and practice it accordingly.

Symbolic Interaction

What label or **stereotype** can we put on religion in America today? That is the question a sociologist would ask. We want to know what Americans as a society and people are feeling and how they are interpreting their culture. Religion is impressive to each of us; however, for Americans as a whole, what does it mean? It means that we can express ourselves in individual ways. We can choose to idolize one God, many Gods, or even no God. We may aspire to be one with nature, the mountains, and the earth. Or we can get lost in contemplating life's meaning through deity, science, or hypothetical assumptions of our beliefs.

Health Care and Medicine

Functionalism

Health care and medicine is functional in society today because it helps us experience greater longevity than years past. Medicine has transformed the human lifespan and quality of life. Health care provides prevention and intervention. If a person experiences shortness of breath we call 911 and get help in record time. Health care and medicine saves peoples' lives. This field employs doctors, nurses, and staff in large numbers. This will be particularly true in the next ten to twenty years as baby boomers retire and expand the needs of services for the older generations.

stereotype

Living longer is the **norm** for American society. We can exceed the years of life our parents and grandparents lived. Conversely, there will be a need of researchers in the fields of DNA, pharmacology, and medicine to help transform lives. Childhood cancer has not been eliminated, but children with cancer are living longer lives to the advances of medicine. Men and women with cancer are surviving.

Conflict

Health care and medicine keep us alive longer, but sometimes the quality of life is lower than what is to be expected. Have you seen someone in a hospital or nursing home living each day a life that most of us would never want to be in or even experience? If you do not have a living will, then loved ones can keep you alive against your wishes. Many people have been hurt physically, emotionally, and socially by modern medicine and health care. Unnecessary surgery and medicine can be lethal and irreversible.

Lawsuits over medical errors have elevated the cost of insurance and health care. Private health care companies select the types of care they want to cover. Health care is health care. What medical issues are more important than another? Not everyone has health care in the United States—a sad fact in a country where equality for all is the central component. If health care is not a priority in our lives what does that say about American society?

The conflict here is power and control over individual lives. If an individual cannot afford health care or get access due to lack of resources such as health care through the workplace or lack of money, then it seems that equality is not a priority for our country. Yet, in the long run, we all pay for each other's health care and consequences, no matter how we look at it.

In the field of health care we see the disparity of social class between those who make a lot of money and others who work long and arduous hours for much less pay, including health care workers and certified nursing assistants who take care of the disabled and elderly. American health care workers work long hours while trying to raise a family and complete a college education.

Symbolic Interaction

Health care and medicine in the United States raises a mixed signal: On one side is the idea that health care is a privilege; on the other side is the premise that health care is necessary and mandatory. Of course, there are people who may not side either way. If we look at U.S. health care we know it is expensive. Neither can many afford quality health care on their own nor have a job to get access to health care. The cost to assure every American health care is immense, but not providing free or reduced-cost health care to each American citizen leads to poor health and lack of prevention and intervention. In other words, it costs society more not to give citizens health care than it would to provide it.

Military

Functionalism

The social institution of the military is functional in our society as it provides protection for American citizens. The military also employs many individuals and provides resources to them and their families. The military gives back to the community in times of need and during traumatic disasters. We have a strong military team including the U.S. Army, Navy, Air Force, Marines, National Guard, and Coast Guard. We have security at airports, state patrols, and the local police. Protection of American citizens is the goal and objective of these institutions. Without these military institutions, citizens would be at risk of chaos. The military units supply order and structure for society to flourish.

Conflict

The military is a conflict for a few reasons. The military can invade countries that may not want help. Soldiers leave families behind for years at a time. Death can be eminent for soldiers who make the ultimate sacrifice out of loyalty. We could look at the deaths of soldiers in combat as heroic, but for the most part it leaves families, friends, and loved ones changed forever. Soldiers and their families are not paid much—they are actually paid more for being deployed than remaining in the states. Soldiers risk future relationships when they're deployed for long durations, as they lose time shared with loved ones and friends.

Symbolic Interaction

The symbolic representation of the military is that it protects and defends our country. The military as an American institution at times represents to the people power and loyalty to freedom and democracy. When a soldier is seen in uniform there is a sense of pride for the country and liberty. After 9-11 we knew that the military was our defense in future attacks. The military poses a strong sense of security and sphere of influence. We are proud of our military. We wave the American flag on the Fourth of July, raise statues in Washington, D.C. in memoriam, and bury U.S. soldiers in Veteran's National Cemetery to honor their dedication to this country.

Media

Functionalism

technology

American society cannot operate without the social institution of the media. We live each day with **technology** in our hands at work and in our daily endeavors. As a professor I see an increase of students with new smart phones and laptops in class. I do not mind them bringing these technologies to class as long as they are considerate of the learning environment. I am one to take out my new iPhone when in meetings and conferences wanting to check emails, the Internet, and to get work done. It is the new normal for our society today. We cannot market media at large and then expect it not to be a part of one's life. I recently showed a video in class. I went to the back of the room and noticed everyone in the back row had a phone on their desk checking it on occasion. I was doing the same. My 5-month-old granddaughter is using an iPad2 already, preferring that over the new iPhone.

Numerous citizens are making money using and marketing technology. This is functional for those who are getting paid and for those who are using the new technology. As I sit here and write this book on my laptop I am also watching a movie on a big screen TV while texting my son in another country. This is incredible! Why wouldn't we buy this new technology? VHS has transformed to DVD and Blue-ray. Netflix and Redbox spares us the costs of buying a movie for twenty bucks. As we watched the inventions transform into organized assets, society changed, and we experienced progress. Nothing has changed but the technology; however, we are pleasantly entertained by the facets and deliveries of the social institution of the media.

Conflict

Conflict perspective focuses on power, control, and competition. Technology, of course, has throughout history been seen as positive, lacking any response to conflict. Money and efficiency have led a supposed transparent trail to unknown consequences. Conflict or indifference has not been the norm for American society and the world as new skills and ideas have transformed society. That said, how is media a conflict in our country when no one really sees it that way?

Media portrays what we need to get, such as an iPhone, a smartphone, DVD player, big screen TV, and even computers. None of us can really afford all these things, but we buy them—and why? The pressure is real for common people who work every day and want the products for their entertainment value. Although most of us cannot afford new technology, we keep buying it at any cost. Who would not be without a cell phone today? I have asked many students in my classes over the years if they have a cell phone. The responses are unanimous. Almost every student has one. And the same goes for computers. Preschoolers and kindergarteners now have computers, even though there is not enough money to support education in general throughout the United States. Who has the money to support new technology in a recession that wants to cut Head Start and kindergarten programs, and K-12 and higher education opportunities?

We pay a large amount of money into media outlets. Maybe technology companies should be donating to the institution of education. Let's face it, our children suffer from lack of resources; yet manufacturers of technology make money from these individuals. For the past twenty years the new skills and knowledge have transformed society, allowing us to experience a new world and new way of life. Yet, there is a greed that has taken over society. If we can make money, then what are the consequences on the common people, which is most of us? Here lies the conflict.

I can remember when the recession and foreclosures burst the bubble in 2008–2011 across the country. The first thing we heard is the blame on the millions of American citizens who signed up for the American dream—that is, a simple house to live in. We were told we knew what we were doing and that none of us deserved to even have a house in the first place. What about the mortgage brokers who were making and faking the money that the homes were worth? What were the profits of those who got American citizens to buy these homes at the highest price ever seen in American history? Who had the power to do this? It most certainly wasn't the common people; it was the corporate and the elite. "Hey," they report, "we are not making enough money, so who can we use for scapegoats to get richer?" All and all, we know the routine. Those who have the power, property, and the prestige continue to make more, as the commoners struggle to stay afloat.

Symbolic Interaction

The media means so much to American citizens today. We are absorbed by the media around the clock: when we wake up, go to work, stay at work, travel home, and relax for the evening. Children unveil their wants to be like singers, rock stars, American Idols, and actresses. Dora the Explorer and Shrek have transformed the lives of young toddlers across the country. Video games, movies, television, and social media are part of what we need and know as part of the American culture. It is an American icon to know the new movies coming out and the new technologies available. I was surprised to hear so many Americans bought the newest iPad. Who can afford it?

theory of cultural lag

William Ogburn presented the **theory of cultural lag**, noting that society introduces new technology but the culture has yet to accept it. This can take a few years, but less years now than before. Technology has changed society faster than any other invention over the past fifty years. Media is a source of comfort to people. Seniors watch their favorite television shows; family members give computers and cell phones to parents and grandparents to symbolize the importance of having one. We are bombarded by new technology that transforms every day of our lives.

Politics

Functionalism

Politics are at the heart of American society. We vote and not vote for the justice and representation of who governs this country. It is functional to have a democracy in society today. People represent the vote. We determine who goes into office by the vote. This is the most functional aspect in U.S. politics. We may view ourselves in a **democratic façade,** where we have the ability to vote but not make it count. Despite this dilemma, we need to vote to stress our opinion or desire for change. If we do not vote, we are allowing the process of those who have the power to move on with their own choices. Voting may seem irrelevant, but is not in any measure.

democratic façade

Politics today continue to provide policy and legislation for the people. Many commoners such as you and me may feel we are not part of this process. In America we are always part of this process based on the Constitution. If we have money we have more power, but as the working class we do have say in politics. We just have to believe that the U.S. democracy works for the common good.

Conflict

Americans sometimes believe their vote does not count. This is the ideology of the conflict perspective proposing that someone has more power over the vote. Average American citizens believe that the people with money and power have more clout to influence the nationwide vote than the average citizen. **C. Wright Mills** (1958) talked about the top 1% of the population who controls societal decisions. He wrote a book regarding this matter, titled appropriately, *The Power Elite.* Mills's work has become quite popular today. What are your ideas on the structure of American and global society as it relates to the **power elite**—that is, the top 1% of the population who have the power and wealth to make most of America's and the world's prominent decisions?

C. Wright Mills

power elite

Symbolic Interaction

Politics can be good or bad depending on who you ask. But, for what it is worth, politics is the reason why many have come to this country and have built a democracy. We reflect the idea of a democratic process "for the people represented by the people." Politics in a country of millions of people can become complex, because of the large number of people involved. You hear those who are sure we have a democracy and those who are sure we do not. However, when we look at the United States and expose its rare philosophy and Constitution we can believe, stay neutral, or not believe. We have a choice.

Election time brings people to respond on the previous notes. We look for leaders who will correspond to our values, who will give us what we are looking for. If we cannot find that in a candidate we are discouraged and even disappointed. Thus we may not care and become empathetic. Here we may not be able to respond to vote.

Economy

Functionalism

global marketplace

The economy is struggling in the United States and in the world today. European countries are impacted by the weak U.S. economy. We rely on each other to survive in today's global market. The **global marketplace** equals imports and exports of goods and services, which marks the function of the economy. We need other countries for exports and imports as much as they need exchange from the United States. If you look back over the past two hundred years, transporting of goods has never been so popular. The trading of goods keeps countries rewarding and prosperous.

Entrepreneurship is the backbone of American society. The American ideology creates trade for selling and buying. Services are exchanged and rendered. There is always a need for the exchange of goods and services. We can help others as they help us. American society has always had the "give and take" mentality of reciprocity. What can I do for you in exchange for what you can do for me? Simply said, it works this way. We get more goods from outside the country while sending our extras to other countries. The diverse array of products is at our feet if we are able to buy them.

Conflict

The disadvantage with buying all the time is not having money when needed. The exchange of goods and services creates a "pocket of wants." Many of the middle- to lower-class individuals in society cannot afford most of the products advertised in the media, yet they buy them despite the lack of money in the bank to support the needs. The idea of credit, insurance, and the like, establishes an irrational ideology of the future. Consumers, such as you and I, continue to ask for the perfect credit score so we can attain the perfect material goods essential for our so-called future.

The common man (i.e., you or I) knows how to work hard in a society of equality; however, the rewards of working do not meet our material demands. Again, we see the electronic gadgets, travel opportunities, homes, and cars we may strive to attain. We dream big, we want the dream quick, and cannot understand the misery most of us subside in since we cannot get it. This is a disadvantage. Middle- and lower-class individuals can dream, but the reality is we cannot attain. When we realize that we are not the rich and the upper class, we can deal with the conflict of aspiring to be more than what we can surmise. Sure, many of us have the opportunities to achieve more, but the fact is it will be fine if we do not. An instant millionaire can drink or gamble himself to death. This is a true conflict. The idea of a conflict is that one powers another. For most of us in American society this is true.

Symbolic Interaction

Money is everything in our society, or at least a dominant theme. We label our lives based on what we can try to achieve instead of what we have achieved. Technology bombards our every whim throughout the media, shopping, and peer influence. The label we put on the economy today is that of weakness and volatility. Many U.S. citizens are unemployed or **underemployed** (working many jobs yet lacking health care insurance coverage, retirement benefits, and job security). An interesting trend in U.S. employment is the pervasive accounts of part-time work with low wages, low job security, and no chance of seniority. The phenomenon is happening in every institution. The country

underemployed

law
social control

as a whole hires more part-timers than full-timers in the workplace. This is the norm for our American society. Permanent stable work is less accessible.

Law

Functionalism

For years the law was based on religious ideals and thoughts. Today in America the law has eluded to policy that works for all. The law protects the innocent and the not so innocent until proven guilty in a court of law. Unjust accusations of people are not tolerated in our society. We have a justice system protecting individuals through due process. Due process allows for evidence to prove or not prove one's fate in the judicial system. Therefore the **law** is defined by the norms put into **social control** and enforced by appointed officials and citizens.

Another function of the U.S. legal system is the ability to employ lawyers, court staff, judges, and others who keep the court and legal system operating. The law protects society from harm. We rely as citizens on the police and the policy of law to establish a comfort ability to be safe in our everyday life. Random acts of crime happen, but because the law is established and present there is no doubt we are being protected in our homes, workplace, and community.

Conflict

There are holes in the legal system especially when it comes to money. If you do not have enough money to hire a lawyer today you may lack the legal efficiency and rationale that each individual in our society deserves. The offenders have many rights today in comparison to the victims. Victims do not have privileges in our society. We do not emphasize enough and look at those who will be psychologically damaged for years due to offenders getting away with acts of violence on adults and children. The criminal justice system is truly geared for the criminal to have protection and due process while victims sit idly by wondering how to deal with the tragedy and horror.

An additional aspect of the legal system is the lack of policy to benefit victims. Offenders at all levels, including institutional and personal, are getting away with lethal crimes against victims. Look at the American citizens who lost their homes, retirement money, and dreams to have what any American wants—a good job with security, savings, health care for the family, and a long life to see their children grow to be parents and grandparents. One act of crime can ruin this pathway for so many people. Not enough human rights, laws, and restitution are in place for victims of crime in the United States today. We fail to prosecute for emotional abuse, which is the underlying foundation of present and future victimizations. We must do more to help victims by providing resources, preventing further victimization to occur, and empowering them versus the criminal—the one who took the power in the first place—by placing control back in their hands.

Symbolic Interaction

What does the law mean to you? What type of label or stereotype represents your idea of the law and legal system in the United States? The legal system invades every aspect of our lives as we are conducted by laws, policies, and legislation. Have you ever wanted to change legislation? This is when your ideas can transform the world. The law is embedded in every institution, from the family to higher education. The United States is hugely populated as stated earlier in the book. Each of the millions of individuals in this country is regulated and controlled by the laws established therein. Today, while you read this paragraph, write down the laws that managed your decisions from the time you woke up this morning to the time you go to sleep. How long is your list of social control policies? The laws deem what is appropriate in society. Laws establish the norms of everyday individual and group functioning. If we know what is wrong in society, then we certainly know what is right; however, the law can be interpreted individually in a positive, negative, or neutral way.

|

Functionalism

science

race

Science is new, in essence. Today we explore novice possibilities through experiment, research, and trial and error. Possibly science can construct inventions, and discoveries of history appear obsolete. For example, for years we had a word for **race** noting physical differences between others to the point that these defining physical characteristics were conditioned with social class, status, and esteem. Race is one thing; social class is another. Through work in DNA, such as the Human Genome Project (supported by the National Geographic Society), we see race and social class have been combined over years of slavery and privilege, keeping the status quo (i.e., the way it has been for years). The Human Genome Project can be found on the National Geographic Society's website, where it shows how we are linked to each other years ago and miles away (National Geographic Society, Human Genome Project, 2012). See how, with the use of science, DNA results, and analysis, we embark on new understandings of our existence.

Society is shifting more rapidly than years past through science. For example, medicine keeps a person alive longer. New hips, hearts, kidneys, legs, and still eyes can give a person a second chance for life. We will discuss in future chapters the sociological perspective on the human developmental lifespan. I have seen children survive cancer in the late 1970s who are now in their forties. The science of medical research and technology kept children with cancer alive through new technology such as surgeries, x-rays to find tumors, and radiation to destroy tumors. Children were given life and a chance for memories to be made. Medicine and science continue to expand our longevity and survival chances. Recently, a family member was hospitalized for possible lung failure. The expansion of new technology kept her breathing through man-made tubes and oxygen in intensive care. A few months more to share with family are immeasurable.

Conflict

A family member can live longer through the expansion of science. Science brings life, but to what expense at times? I mentioned having a family member getting a chance to live longer with the diagnosis of possible lung failure so that the family can spend a few more months together. That is a functional response. The conflict remains the cost of living longer. What is the "quality of life" versus the cost and morbidity to stay alive? Many seniors and individuals are living longer due to technology (i.e., new ideas created in one's thoughts). Each day humans are able to create many new inventions, medicine, and ways of living longer. Seniors have a higher morbidity rate living longer and suffering longer, although this is not indicative of the entire elderly population. Conversely, science has breathed years of new life and chances to experience friends and families for days beyond a prognosis of dismay. Enchanting ourselves with the likelihood of sustaining life through treatment and chronic care appears the correct thing to do, but the ideology of a lengthy existence may substitute for added years of relentless unrelieved poor health and pain. Most of us will spend our very last days in hospital scenery. Where do you want to live your final days? This is a mere example of how science can be used for power and exploitation of financial gain. Gaining profit to keep people alive could be a concept to ponder.

Symbolic Interaction

We explored the functional and conflict aspect of science today. What does science mean to Americans? The idea of having the following swarms our lives without consciousness: cell phones, high-definition televisions, surround sound systems, medicine to escape chronic illness and to subside worries, cars that inhale fuel, mountaintop mining and clearing in the Appalachians, **gentrification**, and the World Wide Web. The access of science may be seen with curiosity, resistance, and the reluctance for **social change**. The truth is, social change is moving faster than ever before. The young embrace the change. The old cautiously endure and adapt to new changes. Science is the essence of alteration for one and all. In one way or another, science will always shape humanity.

gentrification

social change

CHAPTER TWO *summary*

The ten social institutions introduce us to the structure of society. The three sociological theories of functionalism, conflict, and symbolic interaction deduce the objectivity of each social institution. Education, family, religion, health care and medicine, military, media, politics, economy, law, and science display the American social institutions. Each institution is synchronous with every other institution. Education is affected by the economy. The economy is affected by medicine and health care, which interact with religion. Religion and politics intertwine. Politics involves the military. The social institution of the military influences the media. The media and the family effortlessly connect. The family is legally influenced by the law. The law allows for science in certain circumstances. The cyclical connection continues as we express, evaluate, and enter social issues of today.

Please answer the following questions:

1. List five of the social institutions from this chapter. Apply the three sociological theories with real-world examples from your life. Elaborate with full paragraphs and examples.
2. What are your thoughts of the three sociological theories? Please explain in complete paragraphs with examples.
3. Which social institution(s) are the most important to our society and to your own life? Why or why not? Please elaborate with complete paragraphs and examples.

Sociological Key Terms

1. Society
2. Population growth
3. Power and control
4. Competition
5. Value
6. Global market of capitalism
7. Pursuit of profit
8. Social class disparities
9. American culture
10. Ideology
11. "Way to the American Dream"
12. Provided function
13. Modern family
14. Modern religion
15. Ideology
16. Traditions
17. Rituals
18. Stereotype
19. Norms
20. Technology
21. Theory of cultural lag
22. Democratic façade
23. C. Wright Mills
24. Power elite
25. Global marketplace
26. Underemployed
27. Law
28. Social control
29. Science
30. Race
31. Gentrification
32. Social change

CHAPTER *three*

GROUP BEHAVIOR AND SOCIAL STRUCTURE IN OUR SOCIETY TODAY

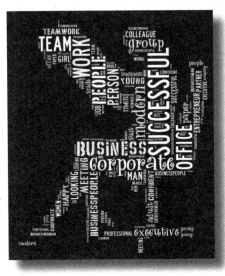

© Isma Riza, 2012. Under license from Shutterstock, Inc.

- Group dynamics
- Primary and secondary groups
- Social structure: Formal organizations, non-profit groups, and bureaucracy

GROUP DYNAMICS

To be in a **group** means to be circled into a philosophical and collective sameness. At the same time, social change has not evolved into modern-day collective change without the resistance from a few. What we may be in one group may differ from what we are in another. **Social connections** appear to be a survival mode. Others look to each other in group settings for consensus of society in order to move forward. Groups gather for many reasons to get tasks done, gain worth, or to exploit others. For example, let's engage an introduction to sociology class group assignment. The professor assigns an in-class group project ahead of time on the syllabus. Students become intrepid, fearful, and even anxiety-induced over the assignment. Some will seek to learn. Others will seek to get through the assignment. Even further, several students will not even show as to feeling the **social inclusion** of being part of a potential group and recluse to embrace any differences. **Social group** activities in college settings are meant to stimulate new learning and resiliency amongst peers. To be **resilient** in the group is to be a listener, an activist, and a doer for the greater good of the group as a whole, not as an individual. However, to be resilient may truly be an individual trait to protect one's self.

© Monkey Business Images, 2012. Under license from Shutterstock, Inc.

CHARLES HORTON COOLEY

Charles Horton Cooley (1864–1929) developed a unique theory called the **looking-glass self**. "It was Cooley's departure from the Spencerian hegemony, his **role distance** from the Sociological

Movement and his immunity from the ideas that bogged down his contemporaries (Small, Ross, and Giddings) that afforded him the opportunity to craft his path-breaking conceptions of the social—the organic view—and his notion of the looking-glass self, his integral idea of the group stemming from his formulation of the **primary group**, and his ideas of social organization" (Jacobs, 2006). "Cooley's unique notion of the social rests on the integration, not the separation or the opposition, of the individual in society" (Jacobs, 2006, p. 23). "Cooley argued that a person's self grows out of a person's commerce with others" (Cooley, 2012).

primary group

The theory of the looking-glass self is, we are what other people think we are. Society influences individuals and individuals influence society. Cooley, in 1902, stated that "**society and the individual** do not denote separable phenomena, but are simply collective and distributive aspects of the same thing" (pp. 1–2). He goes on to say, cleverly, about the society and the individual, "He (individuals) has no separate existence; through hereditary and the social factors in life a man is bound into the whole of which he is a member, and to consider him apart from it is quite as artificial as to consider society apart from the individuals" (Cooley, 1902, p. 3). Here we see Cooley describing the essentials of the micro-sociological theory, symbolic interaction.

society and the individual

Networking is important in our **secondary groups**, formal groups that are goal-oriented such as this sociology class. You are here to complete the goal of finishing this class on your way to other academic goals. You will benefit from secondary groups as you move through your professional careers. My pathway to where I am today is the product of my achievements and the connections in my secondary groups who saw what I accomplished.

secondary groups

GROUP CONFORMITY

When we are in a group our role and behavior are defined by the dynamics of the group. For example, when you are in a college class you may act one way and when with another group act differently. **Group conformity** is making group decisions as a whole. For example, during the first years of colonial America, in the 1600s, Europeans and Native Americans came together. Europeans, as

group conformity

a group, conformed to the idea that Native Americans were not part of the bigger picture of their new society. Native Americans lost to the Europeans. As a group, the Europeans pushed together to gain the land through war. Four hundred years later we see the pervasiveness of group conformity. Here we see how functional group conformity can be to one group but a conflict for those who are **oppressed**—that is, the exploited group.

Another term important in group conformity is the idea of **groupthink.** Groupthink is the tendency to make decisions in groups even when all parties do not agree. Groupthink theory can be applied to many important decisions a country, government, state, and local county make on a regular basis. The incident of the *Challenger* disaster in 1986 was blamed on the ideology of groupthink. If you have ever had the chance to see a shuttle go up from Cape Canaveral on the east coast of Florida, you know it is breathtaking. People come from all over to view the shuttle launch. The social institution of the media presses for answers when the shuttle is not launched on time. The day of the disaster, engineers and leaders complained and focused on delivery, not engineering and safety issues.

Irving L. Janis's book, *Victims of Groupthink* (1972) reflects on his idea of eight main symptoms (see Chart 3.1).

CHART 3.1 THE EIGHT SYMPTOMS OF GROUPTHINK

1. An illusion of invulnerability, shared by most or all the members, which creates excessive optimism and encourages taking extreme risks
2. Collective efforts to rationalize in order to discount warnings which might lead the members to reconsider their assumptions before they recommit themselves to their past policy decisions
3. An unquestioned belief in the group's inherent morality, inclining the members to ignore the ethical or moral consequences of their decisions
4. Stereotyped views of enemy leaders as too evil to warrant genuine attempts to negotiate, or as too weak and stupid to counter whatever risky attempts are made to defeat their purposes
5. Direct pressure on any member who expresses strong arguments against any of the group's stereotypes, illusions, or commitments, making clear that this type of dissent is contrary to what is expected of all loyal members

6. Self-censorship of deviations from the apparent group consensus, reflecting each member's inclination to minimize to himself the importance of his doubts and counterarguments

7. A shared illusion of unanimity concerning judgments conforming to the majority view (partly resulting from self-censorship of deviations, augmented by the false assumption that silence means consent)

8. The emergence of self-appointed mindguards—members who protect the group from adverse information that might shatter their shared complacency about the effectiveness and morality of their decisions. (Janis, 1972, pp. 191–192)

The eight symptoms that Janis explains clearly note numerous, significant decisions made for the sake of the group. Deadly and tragic consequences can be part of the outcomes. In addition, the people who are in power will influence the idea of groupthink decisions. Nazi Germany demanded social control and led the persuasion of many officers, soldiers, and German citizens to agree to his power, authority, and charisma—so much so that millions of people were murdered. Every day of our lives we deal with decisions that can be very consequential. Understanding the idea of groupthink helps bring awareness to the consequences. The classic Milgram Experiment shows how learners will administer lethal amounts of electrical shock to others just because they are told to is another example of social control. Social class differences denote power

© Mayskyphoto, 2012. Under license from Shutterstock, Inc.

and influence of groupthink in our society today. The few rich have more power to make decisions than the majority of people in the United States and in the world today.

BUREAUCRACY BY MAX WEBER

A **bureaucracy** is a formal organization that gets things done. Why study bureaucracy in society? The reason is there are always

bureaucracy

leaders in a bureaucracy. If we look back at traditional hunting and gathering, and agricultural, societies there was less need for a bureaucracy. In a smaller society, such as the hunting and gathering society, there were a mere 25 to 40 people. As mentioned in a previous chapter, the 2012 census reports approximately 313 million people live in the United States. Bureaucracies then, undoubtedly, replicate institutions of efficiency. Max Weber lived at the turn of the twentieth century when he saw in Europe (specifically Germany where he was born) a growing population from agricultural societies and the beginning of mass production and surplus in the industrial age. The idea of a bureaucracy was to have formal organizations that were task-oriented (e.g., the U.S. government, state identities, and local townships).

Could you imagine the United States and the world today without a bureaucracy? Unfortunately, formal organizations and bureaucracy have grown and worked so well for the wealthy that both have politically and legally gained the title of "corporate personhood" in a Supreme Court decision (*Citizens United vs. Federal Election Commission,* 2010). "Max Weber warned of the dysfunctions of bureaucracy as well as the characteristics of bureaucracy ... Weber noted in the turn of the 20th century bureaucracies had certain characteristics" (as cited in Owens & Valesky, 2011; see Chart 3.2).

CHART 3.2 CHARACTERISTICS OF 20TH-CENTURY BUREAUCRACIES

1. "A division of labor based on functional specialization.
2. A well-defined hierarchy of authority.
3. A system of rules covering the rights and duties of employees.
4. A system of procedures for dealing with work situations.
5. Impersonality of interpersonal relations.
6. Selection and promotion based only on technical competence."

(Owens & Valesky, 2011, p. 69)

I have been teaching Weber's work on bureaucracy for over ten years now. I know he lived in a different time and era than we do, but I can imagine what Weber would say about bureaucracy today. What he did say now (as cited in Owens & Valesky, 2011) is exactly what he said then, that "part of Weber's genius lay in his sensitivity to the dangers of bureaucracy, while at the same time he recognized the merits of bureaucracy in *ideal* circumstances. He emphasized very strongly the dangers of bureaucracy, even warning that massive, uncontrollable bureaucracy could very well be the greatest threat to communism and free enterprise capitalism" (p. 69).

According to Koll (2009), "Henry Richardson suggests a process-based objection to bureaucracy, that is an objection to bureaucracy that does not refer primarily to results, but rather to an ethical flaw that is inherent to bureaucratic procedures" (p. 134). "Richardson is concerned that bureaucratic agencies may have the capacity to impinge on citizens' freedoms in ways that are illegitimate, or arbitrary. That is a threat because in effect the enactment of specific policies that determine how our rights and duties will actually be modified, and if the bureaucracies have more power in making these specific policy decisions, they dominate us" (p. 135). At this point in American history there is no doubt corporations are winning and the poor are losing in a country that promotes equality. As mentioned, corporations have been given rights termed "corporate personhood." The 2010 Supreme Court decision in *Citizens United vs. Federal Election Commission* allows unions and corporations the right to unlimited spending during campaigns and to be considered a "corporate personhood" presenting corporations and unions with an individual citizen right. As American citizens are losing their own rights to equality,

big business is gaining more rights to increase social inequality through legislative decisions like this one. The danger of bureaucracy and formal organizations has taken "a human form."

NON-PROFIT ORGANIZATIONS

Non-profit organizations in America emerged to help supplement need in society. For example, the American Cancer Society has been around for years. Cancer has not been cured, but due to this voluntary organization, they have raised millions of dollars for research and for helping children and families who are diagnosed with cancer. What are some of the non-profit organizations in your area? Are you part of one of these non-profit organizations? Do you volunteer, help with fundraising, or have been a part of fundraising for a non-profit organization? According to the *Palgrave Macmillan Dictionary of Political Thought* (2009), **non-profit organizations** are defined as:

non-profit organizations

> The term of US law to denote institutions run by a board of unpaid trustees, which devote their funds and receipts to causes of general public concern, and which are forbidden by law to make a profit. Donations to non-profit organizations are tax-deductible, and the category is wider than that of charity in English law, permitting involvement in political research and certain kinds of campaigning. Hence there has been a proliferation of non-profit political organizations in the US, often in the form of policy think-tanks, such as the Hudson Institute and the American Enterprise Institute.

The importance of understanding non-profit organizations in sociology is to demarcate the structures that police and govern our societies. Persons versed in program evaluation analysis, such as sociologists, want to examine the structures of society through observing how organizations work (formally or informally). Every day we encounter the policies and structures at work, school, while paying bills and taxes, or even obtaining the birth certificate of our child. We are overwhelmed by bureaucracy and bureaucrats alike. Wouldn't it be easier to go back to small-town efficiency in a mass-populated country? Probably not, as the task is too great to undertake. What we can do, however, is hold structures such as bureaucracy and formal and informal organizations to high standards—that is, insist they set the first priority as customer service, and profit last. Consumers need more protection in our new world of global capitalism.

CHAPTER THREE *summary*

This chapter steps into the structures of society from primary and secondary groups to global structures such as formal organizations and bureaucracies. Sociologists view society by looking at the macro-sociological perspective, including dynamic structures that are manufactured by people to be efficient in a large society. Small societies are less in need of such structures. As the population grows, so have the organizations. This is important to comprehend when studying society and the individual. We can change organizations and policy and this affects the individual and society. Program evaluation is essential in sociology (please see the next chapter on social science research and methods). Sociologists cannot view society objectively without understanding all parts, macro- and micro-sociological views.

Please answer the following discussion questions:

1. Think about the groups you are in. Make a list of the primary and secondary groups you encounter each day. How do you act differently in each of these groups? Please give specific examples.
2. Choose a formal organization or bureaucracy that you would like to write about. List Weber's characteristics of the bureaucracy. Provide examples of how each characteristic vividly displays how it could be functional or a conflict.
3. Choose one non-profit organization in your local county. Either interview the director of the organization or research it online. Write a two-page paper on your interview or research of this organization. Please protect the confidentiality of the non-profit organization by not presenting names of individuals who work there.

Sociological Key Terms

1. Group
2. Social connections
3. Social inclusion
4. Social group
5. Resilient
6. Looking-glass self
7. Role distance
8. Primary group
9. Society and the individual
10. Secondary groups
11. Oppressed
12. Groupthink
13. Bureaucracy
14. Non-profit organization

CHAPTER four

SOCIAL SCIENCE RESEARCH AND METHODS

© Christy Thompson, 2012. Under license from Shutterstock, Inc.

Before commencement in a graduate program of sociology one must be heavily acquainted with the research method. The research method is the objective way of doing research so other researchers will be able to decipher and interpret the results. Statistics are used for many research projects in sociology. We tend to lean toward **quantitative methods**, the use of numbers and data such as surveys and random samples. Only at times will you see research in sociology that is a **qualitative method** involving content analysis, interviews, and observations. Sociologists are social scientists observing group behaviors, attitudes, similarities, and differences.

QUANTITATIVE ANALYSIS

*quantitative
method
qualitative
method
hypothesis
independent
variable
dependent
variable*

In a quantitative study a **hypothesis**—an assumption made to be tested through observation, research, and analysis—will be used to test the relationship between two variables, the **independent variable** and the **dependent variable.** The independent variable *cannot* be changed at the time of the measurement. The dependent variable *can* be changed as the independent variable changes. For example, say we would like to find out the relationship between low-income socioeconomic status and one's level of academic achievement. The hypothesis could be reflected in the following scenario.

Children in high poverty neighborhoods are less likely to finish high school. The independent variable would be the high school completion rates. The dependent variable would be the rate of poverty. As the rate of poverty changes in a neighborhood, then in essence according to the hypothesis, the levels of high school achievement will be lower. Of course, we could reverse this hypothesis. We could say children in low poverty areas are more likely to graduate from high school. How can we obtain data to this nature? First, we can look at the two variables, children who live in poverty and high school completion rates. Most counties obtain data of the children's income levels and achievement rates, and is public information as mandated by the state. Analyzing data that has been previously presented is called **secondary analysis.**

As a graduate student in sociology, I used the General Social Survey (GSS), a nationally represented **random sample.** A random sample is an unbiased sample (e.g., every other person or every thousandth person), so that everyone has an equal chance of being represented in the sample. Let's take a look at the GSS. The National Opinion Research Center (NORC) distributes and produces this **survey**. The NORC is located at the University of Chicago and is the longest running project (NORC, 2012):

> The General Social Survey (GSS) is one of NORC's flagship surveys and our longest running project. The GSS started in 1972 and completed its 27th round in 2008. For the last third of a century the GSS has been monitoring societal change and the growing

complexity of American society. The GSS is the largest project funded by the Sociology Program of the National Science Foundation. Except for the U.S. Census, the GSS is the most frequently analyzed source of information in the social sciences.

In Chart 4.1 you will see the many questions that are asked in an interview to respondents who participate in the General Social Survey. The latest GSS was done in 2010. Some questions remain the same, some are removed, and new ones are added. The GSS is a quantitative analysis using a survey to assess national attitudes. The importance of understanding national attitudes is to reflect the voice of the people in a democracy such as the United States. Why do you think it is important to understand people's attitudes?

CHART 4.1 THE GENERAL SOCIAL SURVEY: 1972–2006

TOPICS
Education

1. What is the highest level of education?
2. What is the highest grade in elementary school and high school that (you/your father/your mother/your husband/wife) finished and got credit for?
3. Did you/he/she ever get a high school diploma or GED certificate?
4. Did you/he/she complete one or more years of college for credit (not including schooling such as business college, technical or vocational school)? If so, how many years did you/he/she finish?

Social Mobility
1. Compared to your parents when they were your age now, do you think your standard of living is much better, somewhat better, about the same, somewhat worse, or much worse than theirs was?
2. When your children are at the age you are now, do you think their standard of living will be much better, somewhat better, about the same, somewhat worse, or much worse than yours is now?

Mental Health
1. Now thinking about your mental health, which includes stress, depression, and problems with emotions, for how many days during the past thirty days was your mental health not good?
2. During the past thirty days, how many days did your poor physical or mental health keep you from doing your usual activities, such as self-care, work, or recreation?
3. On the whole, do you think it should or should not be the responsibility to provide mental health care for persons with mental illnesses?

4. Earlier (in the study), we talked about various areas of government spending. Since we've been talking about the mental health area, please indicate whether you would like to see more or less government spending in the area of mental health care. Remember that if you say "much more," then it might require a tax increase to pay for it. (The responses included spend much more, spend more, spend the same as now, spend less, spend much less, not applicable, and can't choose.)

Economic Policy
1. On the whole do you think our economic system is best, okay but needs some tinkering, needs fundamental changes, needs to be replaced, don't know, or not applicable?
2. On the whole do you think it should or should not be the government's responsibility to reduce income differences between the rich and the poor? (Responses included definitely should be, probably should be, probably should not be, definitely should not be, can't choose, not applicable.)
3. Do you favor government to control prices through legislation?
4. Do you favor government to control wages?
5. On the whole do you think government should provide jobs for all?

© Stuart Miles, 2012. Under license from Shutterstock, Inc.

As you can see the General Social Survey covers many topics (Chart 4.1 only mentions a few). Using a national random sample we have the ability to **generalize** as to Americans' attitudes on social issues, problems, and most of all on social policy. If we can look at the data from a random sample we are assuming that during the **methodological process** researchers in social science understand **validity** and **reliability** when using a national survey like the GSS. Validity is the extent to which the questions in the survey measure what is intended to be measured. Reliability is being able to use the questions in the study repeatedly with precision. The GSS has proven over thirty years the ability to be highly valid and reliable.

PROGRAM EVALUATION

We mentioned in Chapter 3 on groups the idea of bureaucracy, non-profit, and for-profit organizations. As sociologists you might be asked to do a program evaluation of one of these programs. For example, let's take a look at a state-mandated battering program for violent offenders. A state-mandated battering program is to counsel violent offenders in typically six months to a year. To do a program evaluation of the organization (a non-profit, as it is funded mostly by donations), a sociologist may be asked to evaluate the program using a cost-benefit analysis, and comparing goals and objectives with its success rate. I would assume a program that rehabilitates at least *one* violent offender would be a success, but that is not the case. First of all we would need to define "success." Would it be a 25%, 50%, or even a 99% success rate if the offender completed the program in a satisfactory manner? What would you assess as being successful? Since a mandated battering program for violent offenders minimally funds the program by state grants, a program evaluation from an outside consultant (such as a sociologist) will have to conduct the evaluation in a value-free and unbiased manner.

MAX WEBER AND *VERSTEHEN*

In Chapter 3 we explored Max Weber and his work on bureaucracy. Weber is also known for the application of what he called **verstehen**, or value-free research. According to Michael Martin (2000) in his book, *Verstehen: The Uses of Understanding in Social Sciences,* "Weber cautions that, in order to accept a meaningful causal relation in sociology, as a true account, more than rational explanatory Verstehen is needed, that is, more is needed than understanding the actor's behavior in terms of the actor's purposes and motives ... Without empirical verification by statistical methods, statements of such causal relations are only plausible hypothesis; they should not be accepted as true" (p. 19). **Empirical studies** and **facts** are based on the value-free and unbiased interpretation of the scientific method. We cannot assume the truth. We must investigate the obvious as a detective would investigate a case.

Let's go back to the mention of a program evaluation in sociology. A sociologist who is hired to assess an organization as a mandated battering program needs to apply *verstehen,* questioning in a methodological process to analyze the data, not just understand the program. First, a random sample can be taken of the offenders' demographics (e.g., married, income, age, race, ethnicity, religion, number of children, and substance abuse). Now part of the program evaluation is looking at the year's goals and objectives. **Goals** describe the mission statement. For example, a goal could be the following:

goals

> The goal of this mandated battering program is to counsel batterers, lower recidivism rates of violent crimes in the county, and increase success rates (which unmistakably would need to be defined more here).

objective

Then you can go a step further stating the clear, direct **objective**, the specific numbers to achieve stated below:

> The objective of this program for year 2013 is to bring two more counselors in to group therapy, lower the recidivism rates of violence in the county, and increase the success rate of the program by 30%. After you can put together a report of observations of administration, budgeting, marketing, and group therapy with a comprehensive cost-benefit analysis of the program stating where the program needs

fine-tuned

to be **fine-tuned**—that is, assessed on a yearly basis to make improvements and adjustments to the program. This is essential for all organizations to be successful and to be held accountable.

QUALITATIVE RESEARCH—A LESSON FROM JONATHAN KOZOL

KEY TERMS

Sociologists occasionally experiment with observational studies and interview studies, a *qualitative* approach to social science. Jonathan Kozol, an investigative journalist, mastered the art of qualitative studies. He analyzed the homeless. Now you may ask, "Isn't that **bias** and/or **unethical** as the homeless people are not aware of being observed?" Yes, it is. That's why sociologists, for the most part, are trained in numerous graduate programs in sociology with a primary focus on the quantitative method instead of the qualitative method. Biased it may be, but Kozol has brought much to the discipline of sociology. Kozol wrote an article after observing the homeless, called "Are the Homeless Crazy?" published in both *Harper's Magazine* and the *Yale Review* in 1988. In his essay he mentioned the terrible plight and stigma given to the homeless, specifically families and children. Kozol notes:

bias
unethical

> "While conceding that a certain number of the homeless are or have been mentally unwell, they believe that in the case of most unsheltered people, the primary reason is economic rather than clinical. The cause of homelessness, they say with disarming logic, is the lack of homes and of incomes with which to rent or acquire them." (Kozol, 1988, p. 17)

Kozol's website (www.learntoquestion.com) displays his work over the years. He has been an elementary school teacher in the urban areas of Boston observing the plight of children who are destitute. Schools lack funding in urban areas and the blame for being homeless and poor is put on the people. Kozol, on the contrary, has remarked on this false statement, advocating for children through his writings. One of his books, *Savage Inequalities* (1992), goes into detail about the **social conditions** children are facing in America. The title speaks for itself. Through his qualitative observations Kozol has opened the particulars of the poor in American society, as a sociologist and an investigative journalist.

social conditions

© Sharon Day, 2012. Under license from Shutterstock, Inc.

CHAPTER FOUR *summary*

As a sociologist you become a social scientist subjected to the *laws of the methodological process*. A random sample gives everyone an equal chance of being represented so that a generalization can be made. The General Social Survey does just that by obtaining collected data on the attitudes of Americans in numerous areas. We can look at trends through the use of a **cross-sectional analysis**, done in one year or comparing years in a **longitudinal study** over the years. Either one of these studies provides interesting and important information on the norms in society when done in a national random sample. Generalizations can only be made to the **target population** being considered.

cross-sectional analysis
longitudinal study

target population

Weber's use of *verstehen* establishes more than understanding the social issues, but to go beyond the obvious to explain the unobvious. Implicit assumptions, such as covert stereotypes, do not work for social science research. Sociological research and methods are needed to find the less obvious variables that may exist. Independent and dependent variables make up the hypothesis to be investigated. In the social sciences, research is not what you expect, but what you do not expect. Data collection through interviews, surveys, random samples of target populations, and observations guide sociologists to scrutinize even the most operative studies. We must define and use **operational definitions,** precise definitions to measure. Research must be valid and reliable knowing what we are measuring is true and consistent.

Program evaluation can be used to examine organizations from outside consultants such as sociologists on an annual basis. A cost-benefit analysis, data collection, and observations can be added into the program evaluation to report how a program has met goals and objectives. Recommendations are made from the sociologist (consultant) to what may be needed to change or fine-tune for the upcoming year. Through this report grants can be written to gain financial funds desperately needed to run important community programs.

Kozol is an advocate for children, the poor, and the bettering of society. He has mentioned to the country the devastation that lack of funding has done to our American children and families living in poverty. Money has been cut to schools that are not producing higher scores from students and teachers when in fact the scores are there to describe the necessity of *funding more, not less*. His work on the homeless in urban areas brought mandatory attention to the matters of the poor when many blame their plight. In the volatile economy we are in and the rising of the number of children in American schools, this is not the time to cut educational funding. Education is the key for our children's success and productivity and our America's future as a thriving and prosperous country. Qualitative and quantitative research can help show what is really going on in the United States.

Please answer the following discussion questions:

1. Pick a topic to study about our society. Write a few hypotheses to describe your study. What are the independent and dependent variables? What type of qualitative or quantitative methods would you use for your study? What would be the target population? Who could you generalize to? Please be specific and elaborate with examples.

2. Choose and read a writing by Jonathan Kozol. Write a one-to two-page analysis of the literature, being critical of the research and findings presented. Use direct examples from the writing using citations and APA format. What were the key points of the writing? Did you agree or disagree, and why? How is the writing by Kozol applicable to the world we live in today? Why is the research important?
3. Select a local organization of your choice. What are the goals and objectives of the organization? Propose a complete program evaluation including how you would collect data, analyze the data, develop a cost-benefit analysis, and make recommendations to fine-tune the organization for the next year.

Sociological Key Terms

1. Quantitative methods
2. Qualitative methods
3. Hypothesis
4. Independent variable
5. Dependent variable
6. Secondary analysis
7. Random sample
8. Survey
9. Generalize
10. Methodological process
11. Validity
12. Reliability
13. *Verstehen*
14. Empirical studies
15. Facts
16. Goals
17. Objective
18. Fine-tune
19. Bias
20. Unethical
21. Social conditions
22. Cross-sectional analysis
23. Longitudinal study
24. Target population
25. Operational definitions

CHAPTER *five*

DEVELOPMENTAL SOCIOLOGY

© Andrey Arkusha, 2012. Under license from
Shutterstock, Inc.

SOCIALIZATION

Sociology is an important topic as it teaches us early on our role in society. We begin in our early years of life perceiving the world as it is introduced to us. The **socialization process** begins at the moment of conception. The womb becomes the first social environment we interact with. A pregnant mother is surrounded by society influencing the child's growth. Socialization is similar to Charles Horton Cooley's theory, the looking-glass self. The **social environment** we live in influences our self-perceptions.

*socialization
process*
*social
environment*
*social
development*

*developmental
psychology*

The home we live in, the people we see, the media we watch, and the material and nonmaterial culture influence every part of our **social development**.

Developmental sociology is defined as understanding the world around us and our role in it that determines our own self-identity. Developmental sociology is a new discipline that can be compared to developmental psychology. **Developmental psychology** determines the biological, emotional, social, and psychological trends that happen to an individual on average throughout one's lifespan. So you ask, "What is the difference between the social aspects of developmental psychology to the novice discipline of developmental sociology?"

Well, developmental sociology considers all aspects and influences in a person's environment as a whole. Is the individual aware of his or her surroundings in the social environment? How do social surroundings make individuals who they are? How much are they aware of the influence in their surroundings? And, most of all, what is their ability to cope and to deal with stresses, to be **resilient** in everyday living?

Resiliency is fascinating in the manner it develops throughout socialization in the early years of existence. The foremost five years of being are vital in gaining a moral conscience and awareness of life. In developmental sociology it is the idea of being resourceful and to have choices to make decisions. A child or an adult should never have to make a decision without knowing what the significant possibilities are. Resiliency is a lifelong endeavor as is socialization. When you are in the elder years, resiliency will be essential to aging successfully. I would like to add we become resilient from making every kind of decision, good or not so good. To be resilient one must not look at the "not so good" decisions as failures. This is counterproductive to building a resilient child and even a relationship with others. Let's go to the research on resiliency to comprehend the field of developmental sociology.

In an article written by Bonnie Bernard (1997), titled "Turning It Around for All Youth: From Risk to Resilience," she states that "social science research has identified poverty, a social problem as the factor most likely to put a person 'at risk' for drug abuse, teen pregnancy, child abuse, violence, and school failure ... Even though this approach sometimes succeeds in getting needed services to children and families it has led to stereotyping, tracking, lowering expectations for many students in urban schools, and even prejudice and discrimination" (p. 1). Bernard also points out one of the most critical aspects of teaching, nurturing, and guiding children: "Looking at children and families through a deficit lens obscures recognition of their capacities and strengths, as well as their individuality and weakness ... The starting point for building on students' capacities is the belief by all adults in their lives, in their school that every student has inner resilience ... to recognize the source of their own resilience" (p. 1). I could not have said it any better—this is the importance of social abilities in adults to help develop children's social abilities. I always emphasize we get through our weaknesses (and we all have them) by recognizing our own strengths and achievements (and we all have them). "Resilience skills include the ability to form relationships (social competence), to problem solve (metacognition), to develop a sense of identity (autonomy), and to plan and hope (a sense of purpose and future)" (Bernard, 1997, p. 1). Each child deserves this chance to learn to be resilient from resilient leaders, parents, teachers, relatives, friends, and mentors.

Child development should include opportunities to develop resilient skills by making choices on one's own and learning from consequences. Of course, the age of a child is critical here. You would not introduce social situations to children inappropriately (as is the case for victims of child abuse and neglect which we will talk about next in this chapter). We can provide an example of a 10-month-old infant who receives three different types of table food. The infant has a choice of the three types of food. The infant will choose from feeling, tasting, and smelling the items to eat, making a decision to eat what he or she prefers. Future choices may become easier as the child has chosen before and learned from the choices made. Another example would be a 2-year-old choosing not to eat a peanut butter and jelly sandwich for lunch, but is adamant to eat dessert first. What would be the best way for the child to learn resilient skills in this situation? The choices clearly are to give the child the dessert before eating the peanut butter and jelly sandwich or maybe wrap the sandwich up and place in the refrigerator for later. What would you do? Think about the consequences of each choice for the child.

Another example of developing resiliency in children is going to school. Many young people have social anxiety about going to school. For children in poor urban areas this is even more so. Parents may choose what is best for their child. Let's look at an adolescent who does not want to go to high school the first year transitioning from junior high school. The adolescent notes to the parent, "I want to be home-schooled." What decision can a parent make to help the child use this as a lesson of building resiliency? The two choices are clear, home-school or go to high school. What choice would you make? Well, let's think of the child interacting with other students who are just as nervous as they are or remain home unexposed to the dynamics of public education, a true social condition that a child can grow socially with one's peers. I am not an advocate for home-schooling when it comes to providing the optimal social environment to build resiliency in children.

Resiliency is not often talked about in our society. From a sociological perspective, resiliency is symbolic in that there is social interaction. Resiliency is learned through responses with others. At the functional level, resiliency in an institution or even society has to foster all people in the community, the rich and the poor. As Emile Durkheim noted in societies that were chaotic and less socially integrated, higher suicide rates were evident. As a functional theorist, Durkheim explained the macro-sociological perspective on creating socially integrated communities. I would like to call them **resilient communities.** In contrast, the conflict theory at the macro-sociological level states societies lack norms, or experience **normlessness**, as Durkheim relates. Karl Marx, conflict theorist, would explain reasons for societies with normlessness to create **inhibiting resilient communities**. The importance of resiliency is twofold: (1) Symbolically, the individual creates consequences through social interaction as a function or conflict, and (2) societies create consequences that can lead to resilient or inhibiting resilient communities. Patterns of social interaction at the individual level as well as at the societal level lead to individuals and societies to optimize possibilities and resources or quit and give up on the future. As we look at our economy today in America and in the global marketplace we can apply Rutter's (2012) statement on resiliency: "Equally, they

resilient communities

normlessness

inhibiting resilient communities

may be resilient in relation to some kinds of outcomes but not others. In addition, because context may be crucial, people may be resilient at one time period in their life but not at others."

For example, Barbara Witherspoon, new principle of Atkinson Academy in New Hampshire, wrote ten years ago of her leadership to use resiliency, to build on one's strengths throughout the community, and to develop plans to rebuild the school's success. Witherspoon (2012) wrote on resiliency in the introduction of the book, *School Wide Approaches for Fostering Resiliency,* where she discusses her situation, "as we studied the resiliency-building information, we have seen it also applies to adults. Applying the resiliency framework to students and adults has taken learning on my part, as I have a tendency to push too hard and be too impatient ... I am learning to walk my talk; to respect each person in the school as an individual, to discover each person's strengths and how best to foster his or her resiliency." The consequences of building resiliency in teachers, families, and American children can reach success of rates of social development strengthening children, families, schools, and society.

CHILD ABUSE AND NEGLECT IN AMERICAN SOCIETY

For over a decade I have been teaching the social problem of child abuse and neglect in our society. As we took a look at the new field of developmental sociology we see that our focus as a society is not on building resiliency in children; this lack of ability to demonstrate resilience for our families and children has severe consequences. People may have limited resources due to the economy, but we can still improve on fostering resilience for every child in America. Most introductions to sociology textbooks in the socialization chapter discuss feral children, social agents such as parents, families, and religion, and the alarming statistics of child abuse and neglect in the United States today. I am taking a new approach using my background in domestic violence and lifespan development to focus on strategies to rid the country of child abuse and neglect, a part of developmental sociology.

In sociology we converse with reference to prevalence rates and the incidence rates of child abuse and neglect by definition, meaning how often it happens and to what extent. As we learned in Chapter 4 on social science research and methods, we must operationalize a definition to measure it. Measuring resiliency would be the same way. The University of New Hampshire's Family Research Laboratory under the guidance of the Department of Sociology has been one of the foremost social science researchers on the welfare and health of American children. The research in this area is critical and necessary. In developmental sociology I would like to combine the research on resiliency (and the lack thereof) in helping children with real strategies for building parents and children's resilience, focusing on a plan to have resiliency building in schools, home, and in the community. We as a society tend to focus on the consequences only after negative events happen to us. In contrast, resiliency is an everyday process, empowering all people, especially families and children, to survive optimally. (Note in Chapter 7 we will focus more on victimology and deviant behavior.)

So the question here as a sociologist is, what can we do to increase resiliency? As Witherspoon described earlier, we need to focus on strengths to help children build resiliency. Parents need more from society such as resources to help with poverty; and the last thing we need to do is cut funding to education. The institution of the family and education are the critical, dynamic roles to resilient success. Researchers in aging, or the study of *gerontology* (see Chapter 10), can analyze studies of people age 65 and older who have remained resilient despite their negative experiences of early childhood maltreatment.

gerontology

We will also discuss in Chapter 10 other protecting variables for people who have lived over the age of 65. For ten years I have taught the sociology of aging. I have read close to hundreds of interviews with older adults. Seniors, for the most part, have incredible resiliency and a key into the field of resilience. Numerous interviews I have read have produced unbelievable accounts of abuse and neglect in childhood and exuberant resilient skills in the older years. As noted, the definition of resilience is learning how to cope and adjust to adversity, such as child maltreatment. As an adult we can experience trauma of loss due to illness, tragedy, war, unemployment, foreclosure, and recession. We will all face difficult challenges in our lives, but can overcome them by engaging the social environment around us such as friends, family, teachers, and those we meet on a daily basis.

CHAPTER FIVE *summary*

Child abuse and neglect affect many young people in America. Resiliency in an individual, family, and community needs to be addressed at every level—family, school, and community. Victims of child abuse and neglect can grow to be productive and happy members of society. For many reasons an inhibited resilient community through economic recession and unemployment does not provide the needed resources to help. Questions for sociologists would be how to identify resilient and inhibited resilient communities so that added resources are supplemented until the community becomes resilient. Child abuse and neglect is a social problem, not an individual problem. Sociologists explore this issue to recognize and address the needs of a society.

Please answer the following discussion questions:

1. Define developmental sociology. In two paragraphs explain how the definition of developmental sociology applies to your own life. Start with the first decade of your life, then advance through the second decade, third decade, and so forth. If you are between the ages of 15 and 25, project the next two decades of how you will use developmental sociology concepts such as resilience in your future years.
2. Write a seven-day journal. Express in your writing moments when you were resilient or not resilient each day. Reflect after the seven days in one page your thoughts on the journaling experience.
3. Find a recent case of child abuse and neglect in your community. Read the case and be ready to share the case and your personal reflection and reactions to it. How does resiliency play a key role in learning about this case?

Sociological Key Terms

1. Socialization process
2. Social environment
3. Social development
4. Developmental sociology
5. Developmental psychology
6. Resilient
7. Resilient communities
8. Normlessness
9. Inhibiting resilient communities
10. Gerontology

CHAPTER six

THE IDEOLOGY OF CULTURE

© Mona Makela, 2012. Under license from Shutterstock, Inc.

- Culture
- Cultural relativism
- Traditions, rituals, norms, and taboos
- Subcultures and countercultures
- Ethnocentrism
- American values

American culture is defined as common beliefs, values, and traditions within the country. The U.S. culture is relatively young, as I argue that we are still in the learning process. The new

Europeans landed here traveling in large ships, using foot, horse, and covered wagons to go westward. American Indian tribes from Maine to Oregon lived on this land before Europeans. So if I am going to talk about American culture I must spend some time discussing the tribes of our nation before the Europeans' arrival. Sure, you might say, this is part of American history, which is true. But sociologists look at societies and culture, and compare them to see how relevant earlier periods of time in history contribute to society today.

FIRST AMERICAN CULTURE

Growing up in America I learned little about American Indians and their culture. If you grew up here that may be the same case for you. My great great grandfather emigrated to the Northeast from England. He wrote of playing with the American Indian children as a child. One concept I would like to introduce now is **ethnocentrism**, viewing one's own culture as being the center of everything. Now this is surely a normal reaction when comparing one's own culture to another. Anyone, however, could change their mind. I could decide someday the American culture is not the center of my life and my culture preference. Living in a global world today a person can move to another country and obtain a new culture and way of life. I wonder how many American Indians in this country have moved to another country, as their culture has been literally torn to shreds? I do not settle well saying America is my country as I have grown older. I remember hearing a chief at a powwow in Florida during the late 1990s. He came out at the beginning of the ceremony dressed in his ceremonial tribal wear, rattling and singing. He stopped and said to all of us (and I will never forget his words):

"Welcome to my land. My land is your land."

Where are the American Indians today in this country? Let's take a look. According to the U.S. census (2010), 70% of the Native Americans live in urban areas and prefer to be called by their tribal names (as opposed to Native American) and there are over 500 federally recognized tribes in the United States today. "The population of the American Indian in 1860 was around 250,000 individuals, but today there is close to two million American Indian individuals in the US today" (U.S Census, 2010). American Indians made historical contributions to American culture and to societies around the world.

The roads of America were first trails of the Indians from years gone past. Along with the early paths set by Indians, language has been passed down to present-day American culture, as well as other major contributions. Today American culture lingers with the **traditions** of the American Indian.

AMERICAN CULTURE TODAY

American culture consists of **material culture** and **nonmaterial culture**. Material culture is items that we can actually see such as laptops, televisions, cell phones, automobiles, sneakers, and paper. Nonmaterial culture is an ideology, values, and beliefs. Religion, spirituality, and cognitive thought are examples of nonmaterial culture. When we address the concept of American culture in 2012 there is much to consider. Politics, family, education, media, military, religion, health care and medicine, law, economy, and the media define American culture (see Chapter 2). American values and beliefs are based on the Constitution

material culture
nonmaterial culture

and law; however, American culture involves diversity and continuous change. Every day we encounter new technology in the media, voting of officials to represent American people, unemployment that invades our families' lives, lack of funding and the cutting of jobs for teachers, U.S. military invasions of other countries, protection of the law especially for those who can afford it, freedom of religion, and life-saving medicines with adverse addictive properties. The dynamics of American culture cannot be fully understood without looking at the economics of institutional growth.

cultural lag

Institutional growth in America means to bring the social institutions here to optimal fruition. **Cultural lag**, as stated by sociologist William Ogburn, emphasizes the introduction of new concepts, ideology, technology, and media. However, the acceptance of the new material and nonmaterial items *lags*. Ogburn studied the transformation of society due to new technology. Godin (2010) notes:

> Another forgotten classic is American sociologist William F. Ogburn (1886–1959). Over more than 30 years, Ogburn studied technological innovation through its many effects on society, producing dozens of articles and books. Together with his colleague S. Colum Gilfillan, Ogburn was among the first academics to devote extensive and systematic studies to technological innovation. In fact, with regard to the study of innovation, the sociologists preceded the economists, who in recent years have chosen to concentrate on innovation defined as commercialized invention. (p. 278)

Society and technology are hallmark values in America today. We pride ourselves on all the latest technologies despite the fact that most of us cannot really afford these items. Cable for movies, cell phones for text messaging, wireless Internet to converse with friends and to find new ones, and transportation such as the prominent airplane that has pushed us to a new culture of change, excess, and misery if we do not have the means to achieve the "American dream." **Cultural relativism** is defined

cultural relativism

as the facts of what is really going on in society. For example, we can say American culture has numerous television stations. This statement is culturally relative. If I were to say Americans are obsessed with television, then I am making a judgment, which is ethnocentric. Another example is the statement, "Americans do not work that hard," which is ethnocentric. The fact is Americans work harder than ever before raising children, working, and going to school all in order to buy the American dream.

America is about equality and justice for all. Four hundred years have passed since the birth of this nation. However, women are still oppressed and abused in a dominant patriarchal society. The media of literature, television, and movies portray this each day. Are people watching and reading because they can relate or because it thrills them as entertainment? As a domestic violence researcher the literature is abundant in this area.

THE AMERICAN TABOO: CLASS STRUCTURE

A **taboo** in society is defined as an act that is *unimaginable* to most people in society. In American society we have many **overt taboos** which we openly discuss such as murder, rape, child incest, and cannibalism. However, here in America we have a **covert taboo** that each of us truly believes in the ability to move up in our social class (otherwise known as upward mobility) and to reach the American dream of success and achievement. For most people this is not going to happen. Most of us will remain in the same social class as our former generations due to **inflation**, the rise of prices. This means we do not talk about class structure in American society and the inhibited resilient communities in which we live. American people wish everyday for upward mobility when the evidence reflects the opposite. The American taboo believes in the **American dream** when the majority of workers

taboo
overt taboo

covert taboo

inflation

American dream

will not see this happen. Karl Marx noted in his work, there are only two classes: the bourgeoisie and the proletariat. The bourgeoisie own the "means of production" and the proletariat work for those who own the means. I do not consider anything different when it comes to social classes in America. There are the rich and the poor in our

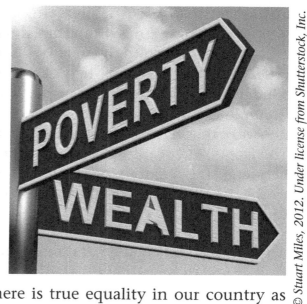

© Stuart Miles, 2012. Under license from Shutterstock, Inc.

American society. Until there is true equality in our country as the Constitution presents, then there will always be the same two classes. Equality is a dream not yet achieved. The American taboo is that we do not mention what I have just mentioned (but I do in my sociology classes). That is, we have a low probability of achieving the American dream, because the lower class continues to struggle after working forty plus hours a week, going to school full time, and raising a family.

AMERICA'S DOMINANT CULTURE, SUBCULTURE, AND COUNTERCULTURE

America's **dominant culture** includes the working class—those who work full time while raising children and grandchildren and going to school to get ahead and embrace the American dream. This is the majority in numbers. However, the working class lacks power and prestige that the upper class elite, the **subculture** of Americans, continue to have. And, if you do not go with the status quo of being submissive to the subculture of America you will be part of the American **counterculture**, going against the norms of society. I am a developmental sociologist, one who sees the social class differences in society as the major source of conflict. Social problems need to be seen as they truly are. One of the most satisfying components of the field of sociology is to know your own life problems are being felt by others. The old saying that "misery loves company" may ring through here. However, we must not sit back and let the small minority—the upper-class rich—dominate an American society that is written into law, "We are all equal." America's norm for its people is that we are all struggling to make ends meet on a daily basis. No one is alone in the dominant culture. By understanding our social class and our relation to society we can bring awareness to social inequalities and try to ameliorate the situations, to make life better in the years to come.

CHAPTER SIX *summary*

American culture is new, pressing forward, and carries taboos that we are forced not to talk about. One thing we tend to not talk about is the idea that we have the real ability to move up in wealth and social class. The fact of the matter is, the majority of Americans will not see an increase in social mobility until this country becomes *truly equal*. Ethnocentrism is considering one's own culture with that of other cultures. It is natural to be ethnocentric, meaning we vision what we are used to and what we know. However, the facts of our culture, cultural relativism, are implicit—we do not talk about things such as social class. My goal in this chapter and in the book is to bring more awareness to individuals on how their dominant group, the working class, is challenged as a whole when it comes to upward mobility. We must be truthful about our social prestige and power. By ignoring that the majority of Americans are poor ignores the reality of our position and power. The elite class in America has the upper hand in marketing to families and the poor the material items we must have in order to be accepted. We keep buying into material culture when we cannot afford it. (I myself am so guilty of this!) When is it going to stop? Is history just repeating itself? American Indians hold on to their own culture, values, and beliefs and the consequences have been astronomical. For example, I recently drove cross-country with my husband and have seen much of the West in the past few years. I was in Oregon and saw an American Indian reservation from the major highway. There were two to three broken-down buildings on less than a quarter acre of land. This is upward mobility in our American culture? I am shamed by how we have taken over North America, how we treat American Indians, and now how the rich are treating American people. If the American Indians can be treated with little respect and almost annihilated, what is stopping them from doing the same to us?

Please answer the following discussion questions:

1. Research one of over 500 American Indian tribes. Describe a brief history of the tribe. What are the changes that have come to them such as location, culture, families, politics, language, and so forth? Please find the number of people in the tribe today. Write at least one to two pages with specific research and examples.
2. List three examples of ethnocentrism and cultural relativism. Compare and contrast the two with real-world examples.
3. In one to two pages explain what American culture is to you by mentioning social class, upward social mobility, and the American dream.

Sociological Key Terms

1. American culture
2. Ethnocentrism
3. Traditions
4. Material culture
5. Nonmaterial culture
6. Cultural lag
7. Cultural relativism
8. Taboo
9. Overt taboo
10. Covert taboo
11. Inflation
12. American dream
13. Dominant culture
14. Subculture
15. Counterculture

CHAPTER *seven*

DEVIANCE AND CRIME

© Kirk Pearl Professional imaging, 2012.
Under license from Shutterstock, Inc.

- Deviance in the United States
- Crime and sociological theory
- Victimology
- A victim advocate system and a criminal justice system
- Functionalism, conflict, and symbolic interaction applied to criminal behavior and social control

Deviance is defined as going against the norms. For example, in Chapter 6 we discussed the importance of recognizing the low probability of achieving the American dream. We do not discuss this in our society as it is considered deviant. If we did speak out about it as I did stating the American dream is not about achieving social mobility, then I may or may not be considered deviant. I am not, however, breaking the law which is a **crime.** A deviant act is not necessarily a crime. A crime, however, is most often deviant. Now I will argue here that if many people in a society do the same, then it may not be exactly deviant. For example, when I was 18 years old, I did what many young people did in 1981 to indicate the milestone of becoming an adult—I went to the jeweler at our mall and got my ears pierced!!! You may notice here how a time period reflects deviance. I felt the need to show my parents I could do something that was deviant, and I did. What did you do when you were 18 that may have been viewed as deviant?

A tattoo, for example, during the 1980s was for the most part a deviant endeavor. For the past five years I have asked students in my sociology class if they have a tattoo and over 50% of the students do have tattoos. Sociologists would not consider getting a tattoo in 2012 as a deviant act. Most college students today have cell phones. If you did not have one you may be considered deviant. Deviance and crime are also culturally relative, meaning what may be deviant in American society may not be deviant in another society or culture. The Musuo tribe of Southwest China practices "walking marriages." A walking marriage is not between a man and a woman, but between many men and women. The Musuo tribe is a dominant matriarchal society where women are the leaders and have the power and prestige to make decisions. The Musuo may be affected by new technology in the next century where "walking marriages" may cease to exist and could be considered deviant.

ATHEISM: A DEVIANT PERSPECTIVE IN AMERICA

Sociologists are prominent researchers on the social institution of religion. Christianity, in its earlier years, was once considered deviant and a crime. Atheism today in America is seen to be deviant. In a country that declares freedom of religion, which was based on not being persecuted for going against the English monarchy, the culture is less accepting of those who do not believe in God, the traditional norm of religion in our American society today. In an article titled, "Becoming an Atheist in America: Constructing Identity and Meaning from the Rejection of Theism," written by Jesse M. Smith (2011) and published in the prominent journal, *The Sociology of Religion*, "sociologists of religion have increasingly taken interest in the topic of irreligion, and several scholars have turned their attention to examining those who claim no religion and/or lack theistic beliefs" (p. 215). Smith did a qualitative study on forty atheists in Colorado by interviewing them. Smith states, "Focusing on the interactional processes and narrative accounts of participants, I discuss the process of rejecting the culturally normative belief in God, and the adoption instead, of an identity for which the 'theist culture' at large offers no validation ... As participants sought more education, they became increasingly skeptical of the religious teachings they grew up with ... Once they viewed their religious beliefs as being challenged by scientific and secular explanations of the world the religious ideas and objects (e.g., the afterlife, the Bible) began to take on different meanings" (p. 215). Sociologists look for societal trends in religion. The General Social Survey (mentioned in Chapter 5) contains a section on attitudinal questions to the American public specific to religiosity, such as how often you attend church services. Smith (2011) describes "social construction of early childhood socialization that may represent our religious preferences."

© Ryan DeBerardinis, 2012. Under license from Shutterstock, Inc.

Sociological theories of deviance and crime include functionalism, conflict, and symbolic interaction. Robert Merton's strain theory applies the functional model in explaining crime. Merton examines the **dysfunctional theory** as a conflict theory as it relates to crime and deviance in contemporary American society. Merton notes if we know what is right in society, then we also know what is wrong. The symbolic interaction perspective provides a small number of theories to give explanation of deviance and crime in American society today. The symbolic interaction theories include differential association theory by Edward Sutherland, control theory by Michael Gottfredson and Travis Hirschi, and labeling theory. Sociologists, criminologists, and victimologists use the theories to apply to the field of research of deviance, crime, and victimology.

© *michael rubin, 2012. Under license from Shutterstock, Inc.*

FUNCTIONALISM: ROBERT MERTON'S STRAIN THEORY

Robert Merton has been noted for his work in explaining why individuals resort to deviance and crime. Merton believed individuals all want to achieve success and monetary gains, but not everyone will do this in a legitimate way such as obtaining an educational degree or working in a societal-appropriate manner. Froggio (2007) states the following about traditional strain theories:

> "The traditional strain theories stated that some individuals are drawn to crime when they are prevented from achieving cultural goals such as monetary success or middle-class status through legitimate channels. The strain theorists argue that, in the US, everyone is encouraged to pursue the goals of monetary success or middleclass status. Lower class individuals, however, are prevented from achieving such goals through legitimate channels. Parents frequently do not provide their children with the skills necessary to succeed at school; the children are sent to low-profile institutions and grow up in troubled neighborhoods. Individuals who experience such an impediment to their goal are under an incredible amount of pressure or strain, and they respond by engaging in crime, violent acts, theft, and drug selling." (pp. 384–385)

Sociologists such as Merton note the value of success as one's goal, but for people who are poor or **underemployed**, they work forty hours a week but the pay does not cover their necessities such as food, shelter, clothing, health care, and transportation. The **underground economy**, getting paid to do illegal activities such as prostitution, drug trafficking, human trafficking, and selling illegal weapons, contribute to a billion dollar industry in America and the world today. The underground economy, unfortunately, is preferred by many individuals in order to obtain financial gain and success. The **black market** is another term for the underground economy. The business of the underground economy is an international endeavor. Many individuals pride themselves in buying and selling in the underground economy. Others, specifically women and children, are forced to work for pimps in these black markets internationally. Barry (1981) expresses "from the standpoint of police investigations and criminal prosecutions, there is an actual hierarchy of underground economic systems ... While many underground systems which traffic goods, drugs, or other services are the subjects of continual

underemployed

underground economy

black market

police scrutiny, investigations and arrests or busts, the traffic of women's bodies into prostitution tends to be ignored by the police" (p. 123). Barry (1981) further notes, "if one were to include the pornography industry, which is an aspect of prostitution (some pornographers in Los Angeles have been convicted of pimping), the economic magnitude of pimping would be considerably higher" (p. 126). Barry explains specifically:

> "For example, the most famous hard core pornography movie *Deep Throat* is estimated to have made $600 million. Its star, Linda Lovelace, has revealed that before she made this film she was forced into prostitution by Chuck Traynor. When she escaped from him he threatened to kill her family, and given the brutality she had already experienced from him, she knew he could and would carry out his threat. Pornography is conservatively estimated to be a $4 billion industry a year." (p. 127)

In Chart 7.1 note the application of functionalism, conflict, and symbolic interaction perspective theories to pimping. A pimp makes a profit, gains status and power, and stimulates the underground economy growth in a functional perspective. Merton comments the dysfunctional **theoretical paradigm**, or theory, enables victimization, exploitation, and slavery. Lastly, the symbolic interaction paradigm describes the social interaction between the pimp and those who work for the pimp. The pimp gains power, prestige, and status amongst peers in the underground economy. If we compare the *society of the underground market* and the *society of the legal and free market* there are similarities to roles that are legitimate and to roles that are not legitimate.

We can even say the same when applying the three theories to both legitimate and illegitimate individuals who own the means of production as Marx described. The conflict perspective here notes victimization, exploitation, and modern-day slavery. Lastly, the symbolic interaction paradigm proposes the power, status, and **prestige**, or occupational status. Symbolic interaction can be applied to two other theories: control theory and differential theory.

CHART 7.1 SOCIOLOGICAL PERSPECTIVES ON PIMPING

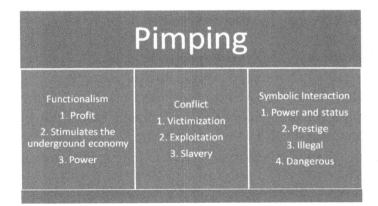

SYMBOLIC INTERACTION THEORY—DIFFERENTIAL ASSOCIATION THEORY, CONTROL THEORY, AND LABELING THEORY

Three theories fall under the symbolic interaction paradigm to analyze deviance and crime in society. Sociologists use the theories to study gangs, juvenile delinquency, familial homicide, child abuse and neglect, child pornography on the Internet, theft, and robbery (just to name a few). **Differential association theory** means "birds of a feather flock together." As we know when using the symbolic interaction approach we are concentrating on microsociology and social interaction. Sutherland first introduced the differential association theory. In a study titled, *The Effects of Mixing Offenders with Non-Offenders: Findings from a Danish Quasi-Experiment,* researcher Linda Kjaer Minke (2011), faculty of law at the University of Denmark, Copenhagen, shows "the effects of mixing offenders with nonoffenders at Skejby half-way house in Denmark" (p. 80). Minke (2011) mentions the results of the study applying differential association theory:

differential association theory

> Skejby half-way house constitutes an outstanding social experiment as offenders are deliberately mixed with non-offenders in order to reduce their risk of recidivism. The treatment group consists of offenders who have stayed at Skejby half-way house while the controls are selected from residents of four other half-way houses. A Cox regression analysis

reveals that the probability of reoffending is 21% lower for the treatment group than it is for the control group. (p. 80)

Differential association theory by Sutherland, a criminologist, can be applied to the results of this study. Offenders in this study are less likely to reoffend if mixed with non-offenders, noting being with people who do not offend can help offenders strive for positive strategies legally. When you think about the people you hang around with are they deviant or not? Are we who we hang around with?

CONTROL THEORY

Gottfredson and Hirschi introduced control theory, which explains we have both inner and outer controls when it comes to making decisions. As a sociology professor and domestic violence researcher my lectures include every theory of deviance and crime. The control theory shows how we make our own decisions based on our social environment. Like the differential association theory the control theory talks about social environment and factors. However, differential association theory describes an individual by the people one associates with. Control theory does the same, but in addition describes the inner controls that guide an individual to make decisions. Control theory can be applied to a person at a party where others are doing cocaine, heroin, or other drugs. One can choose to participate or to leave the party never participating through the inner and outer controls. The inner controls may be one's inner conscience and morals and the outer controls may be the law, parents, teachers, and friends. Of course, the same mentioned people could be part of your inner controls that taught you to be deviant. The use of sociological and criminological theory provides insight to the possibility of explanations proven or disproven. Schulz (2004) states, "Gottfredson and Hirschi's theory of control specifies a lack of control consistent with one's personality ... The authors argue that 'self-control' levels are stable over time which accounts for stable individual differences in crime" (p. 64). The ability to make decisions is based on the inner and outer controls that we have accumulated throughout our life's experiences.

LABELING THEORY

Erving Goffman coined the term **stigma**, a negative label attached to an individual such as thief, pedophile, murderer, and batterer. Once a person obtains a stigma it is difficult to reverse. For example, we can look at famous people in the news like Tiger Woods who are now affected by a label or **stereotype**. Woods has been accused of infidelity with many women during his recent marriage. Before this came out most people knew him for his professional golf career. Former President Bill Clinton reigned for eight years as president of the United States, but not without controversy of his own infidelity. We can apply the danger of using a stereotype on a child such as bully. Our society is tough on children by calling them bullies. I do not see justice in labeling a young child as a bully and having a so-called bully program. Labeling is normal, but hate is not. We should approach discipline behaviors in children with a healthier approach. To label a child a bully is to cast a life sentence as a bully. In working on developing programs for children who misbehave in public education I would heed the warning of labeling a child well before the chance to be developed socially, emotionally, and physically. Children in our society today have much to overcome in a society prevalent in the media, politics, law, economy, health care and medicine, law, military, education, science, and religion. A developmental sociologist would be opposed to placing a label that is so negative during the childhood years.

stigma

stereotype

VICTIMOLOGY: THE VICTIM'S RESPONSE

Sociologists also teach the field of **victimology**, the field of study that focuses more on the victim than the criminal in a scientific approach. Victimology is not a prominent field that many know about. I recently had a class approved for me to teach in this area. My first class on victimology and domestic violence really opened students' eyes to the victim's perspective. I have taught students about victims and victims' rights for over ten years. Teaching an entire class on the discipline covers defining victims and victimology, the reciprocity between victims and criminals, and the lack of advocacy for victims in our society today. Society tends to blame victims for being a victim. For example, a prostitute

victimology

"asked for it" when she was raped or "a wife is supposed to obey her husband." **Marital rape** occurs between spouses; yes, one spouse can say no to the other in the United States. In a traditional patriarchal culture as in the United States, men have power over women, including within married relationships. However, the law is clear that all Americans are protected by the "rape law."

"The National Crime Victimization Survey (NCVS) is the only survey that monitors rape and sexual assault on an annual basis in the United States" (Bachman, Zaykowski, Lanier, Poteyeva, & Kallmyer, 2010, p. 203). The FBI Crime Report is specific to robbery, theft, and murder. Bachman and colleagues (2010) note "national surveys indicate that American Indian and Alaskan Native (AIAN) women have higher rates of rape and sexual assault victimization compared to women from other race/ethnic groups ... Although victimizations against AIAN women are more likely to come to the attention of police, they are much less likely to result in an arrest compared to attacks against either White or African American victims" (p. 203). The NCVS is an informative tracking tool to gather evidence on victimology from the victims' perspective. The NCVS is a nationally represented random sample that asks questions on victimization. The United States, like other patriarchal societies, estimate to hold higher rates of rapes and sexual assaults.

Kirk (2009) notes in the United Kingdom, "The statistics portray a desperately depressing story—it is estimated that somewhere between 5 per cent and 25 per cent of rapes are reported to the police, and of those cases where complaints of rape are made only about 5 per cent end in the conviction of the accused" (p. 281). Kirk (2009) further notes "the labeling of the women keeps the pervasiveness of rape accounts up and prosecution of rape down" (p. 281). The statistics in the United States on rape are also pervasive when it comes to reporting and prosecution. Understanding why this happens in a society is a question for victimologists and sociologists.

Another main issue in victimology is the lack of advocacy for victims. In a system where criminals have rights, the victims render to lesser rights than even the criminal. The U.S. National Center for Victims of Crime posts data from the FBI Crime Reports and the National Crime Victimization Survey. Victimology looks into child victimization rates including child pornography, child abuse and neglect, and child sexual abuse. Elder abuse and neglect is another area within the field of victimology. (We will discuss elder abuse and neglect in Chapter 10 on the sociology of aging.) Victimology is a discipline in need of more dedication and recognition if we are to give victims a voice in society.

CHAPTER SEVEN *summary*

This chapter on deviance and social control explains criminal behavior. In contrast, victimology is rarely viewed and recognized. Deviance is to go against the norms in a society. Deviance is not assumed to be illegal and criminal. However, criminal acts tend to be deviant. Social control includes our inner and outer controls when making legal and illegal decisions, based on our past experiences and personality. Labeling can bring a lifelong stigma on children and should be taken seriously by educators and parents. When we know what is wrong in society, we also know what is acceptable. Advocacy for victims needs more research and media attention. Victims are in need of an increase of advocacy, protection, and support now and in the future. Academic institutions need to integrate classes on victimology and domestic violence to increase awareness of victims' rights and reciprocity. Crimes of victims such as rape, and even marital rape, are less likely to be reported and prosecuted. The stigma for victims is real for men, women, and children. Bully programs in education need to concentrate on a positive collective presentation and program to children throughout every year of education. In conclusion, deviant behavior can be explained by many theories of deviance such as the control theory, the labeling theory, and the differential theory. Sociology explores all paradigms to predict and describe deviant behavior.

Please answer the following discussion questions:

1. What is deviance to you? When were you deviant? Why were you deviant and what age were you? Please provide specific, real-world examples and a reflection in a few elaborate paragraphs.
2. Research the National Crime Victimization Survey and report ten important recent findings from this source. Research the FBI Crime Report and list ten statistics found there. Write a brief reflection on the differences between the NCVS and the FBI Crime Report.
3. Define victimology. Why is there a need for a victims' justice system in America today? Please provide real-world examples and/or statistics. What would you recommend to place a victims' justice system?

Sociological Key Terms

1. Deviance
2. Crime
3. Dysfunctional theory
4. Underemployed
5. Underground economy
6. Black market
7. Theoretical paradigm
8. Prestige
9. Differential association theory
10. Stigma
11. Stereotype
12. Victimology
13. Marital rape

CHAPTER *eight*

SEX AND GENDER IN SOCIETY TODAY

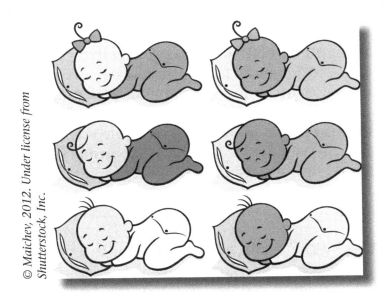

© Maichev, 2012. Under license from Shutterstock, Inc.

- Sex and gender
- Gender and mental health
- Characteristics of patriarchal and matriarchal societies
- Gender inequality

SEX AND GENDER

Sociologists explore sex and gender research to improve and establish the traditions, patterns of male and female roles, and the inequalities that exist in dominant patriarchal societies. **Sex** is biological. **Gender** is cultural and learned. We are born with our sex. We learn our gender. Sex is nature. Gender is nurture. In traditional patriarchal societies such as the United States and the United Kingdom, boys learn to be more aggressive and dominant; girls learn to be pretty and nurturing. When discussing issues of sex and gender in sociology we will also discuss sexual preferences such as being gay, lesbian, or bisexual. The nature versus nurture debate becomes popular when examining sex and gender differences in society.

A study done by Rachel C. Snow in 2007 from the Population Studies Center at the University of Michigan's Institute for Social Research School of Public Health, titled *Sex, Gender, and Vulnerability*, examines the differences in health outcomes by combining sex and gender interchangeably as sex determines gender behavior. Snow (2007) uses "the XX female and the XY male DNA determinants to suggest gender differences in certain health conditions" (p. 2).

Sociobiology understands societal behavior through heredity and genetic determination. Sociobiologists approach male and female differences in health and behavior utilizing an objective approach including both nature and nurture to examine male and female behaviors. Sex differentiation begins in the womb.

Primary sex characteristics include the penis for the male and the vagina for a female. **Secondary sex characteristics** ignite during puberty with enlarged hips and breasts for females and facial hair and voice changes for males. In Snow's (2007) study on health differences in sexes she notes the data used:

> "The aggregate data used for this analysis are taken from the World Health Organization's (WHO) original Global Burden of Disease (GBD 2002) estimates of disability adjusted life years (DALYs) by age, sex and cause, *without age weighting or discounting* (DALYs [0,0]). DALYs provide an aggregate measure of healthy years of life lost due to premature death or disability. These estimates are extremely rough, as they reflect the many extant gaps in regional, and thereby global, epidemiologic data." (p. 4)

In this global study of diseases prominent to females and males we can try to answer and ask questions on sex and gender differences. A global study on health rules out societal factors within nations since all countries do not have the same social environments. "Male estimates of disability adjusted life years (DALYs) that were 25% more than females in 2002 include the five conditions—wars, gout, alcohol-use disorders, road and traffic violations, and violence" (Snow, 2009, p. 7). "Female estimates of disability adjusted life years (DALYs) that were 25% more than males in 2002 include the five conditions—breast cancer, gonorrhea, Chlamydia, trachoma, and migraines" (Snow, 2009, p. 7). More research and questions exist in this data by Snow when comparing sex and gender differences in the world today. We can make assumptions on why females and males experience considerably different illnesses, especially the fact that each have different hormonal patterns released by different reproductive organs. Sociobiologists cannot rule out the variable of the genesis of sex. At the same time, sociologists may want to consider environmental factors in analyzing male and female health outcomes.

© Cartoonresource, 2012. Under license from Shutterstock, Inc.

"Can I be a boy today?"

GENDER AND THE FAMILY

In the United States the family unit is a social institution, according to sociologists. Family in Nordic countries means something different. A study by Ida Oun titled, *Work-Family Conflict in the Nordic Countries: A Comparative Analysis*, describes family dynamics in these countries. "As women's participation in the labor market increased in the Western welfare states during the second half of the 20th century, the ideal of a male breadwinner and a female full-time homemaker became less pronounced" (Oun, 2012, p. 165). She goes on to emphasize, "The increase in women's participation in the labor market has not been followed by a drastic change in men's behavior with respect to household work and childcare" (p. 165). Despite the more active labor market for women in Nordic countries, like the United States, women are doing more of the household chores in a dual-career household. "Empirical studies as well as more theoretical contributions show that social policies influence gender relations and affect the gendered division of labor both within the family and in the public sphere" (p. 165). Oun (2012) notes Nordic families and gender equality:

> "The Nordic countries are often considered to be frontrunners with regard to gender equality, especially regarding the provision of welfare state policies aiming at supporting the reconciliation between work and family life. On the other hand, policy differences within the social-democratic welfare regime regarding the transition towards gender equality have been observed, and previous research has produced divergent results in response to the question of whether the welfare state institutions of the Nordic countries help to reduce work-family conflict. Because of these variations, it is interesting to examine how men and women experience conflicting work-family demands in the different Nordic welfare states." (p. 166)

In a patriarchal society like the United States we may benefit from an increase in gender inequality be absorbing reciprocity between genders without dominance. As we embrace the next ten years in America we need to not assume that females are equal to male. And, much of the research on gender inequality describes the importance of analyzing male to male and female to female pressures to maintain the traditional patriarchal roles that contribute to more years of gender inequality.

CHAPTER EIGHT *summary*

This chapter on sex and gender specifies that sex is what we are born with and gender is learned. In an upper-level sociology class on gender readings and research, the focus is on the sex differentiations and hormones as to the specifics of masculine and feminine behaviors. However, our environment may persuade otherwise. The proof that biology or the social environment is the cause remains elusive. Nature versus nurture is a consideration in sociobiology to determine expected behaviors. Sociologists lean more toward nurture when explaining differences in behavior. We can look closely at the research in gender equality in different nations to make more inferences. The WHO has empirical evidence to validate the nurture component as many women in patriarchal societies have higher rates of mental illness compared to men. In comparison, other cultures and societies, such as the Musuo of Southwest China at Lugo Lake, experience little sexual assaults in their matrilineal or matriarchal society. More research is needed on matriarchal societies to be compared to the dominant patriarchal dynamics in the world.

Please answer the following discussion questions:

1. Write a one- to two-page reflection on your attitudes about sex and gender in our society today.
2. Research the World Health Organization website. List ten key facts and/or points in two to three sentences for each key point.
3. Find a matriarchal society in the world. Research the traditions, rituals, and customs of this society in a one- to two-page paper. In respect to the ten prominent social institutions, how is it different from a patriarchal society? Please elaborate.

Sociological Key Terms

1. Sex
2. Gender
3. Sociobiology
4. Primary sex characteristics
5. Secondary sex characteristics

CHAPTER *nine*

THE MYTH OF RACE AND THE EXPLORATION OF ETHNICITY IN AMERICAN CULTURE

© maxtockphoto, 2012. Under license from Shutterstock, Inc.

- The myth and definition of race in the United States today
- The social construction of race in the United States today
- DNA: the Human Genome Project breaking the ideology of race around the world
- Ethnicity in modern America

RACE AND SOCIAL CONSTRUCTION

Race is a made-up word that is irrelevant and undeniably unable to be proven. For many years anthropologists and sociologists have given a definition of race that includes the physical characteristics of a group of people. However, if color is the description of race, then who makes that determination? Those in power of course are going to decide in their own interests of keeping their status and power. For all purposes of reflecting on the word of race, I use it here only to show how it is irrelevant and invalid. Race is a social construction, as gender is in Chapter 7. As a **social construction** the people in power utilize this word to reflect dominance, exploitation, and even the tragedy of **slavery**, the buying and selling of people based on the supposed color of their skin. Slavery has been used to help people profit through free labor. For example, during the slave period of early colonial America people were bought and sold, a true **genocide** of groups of people.

White Europeans dominated early colonial America, killing and enslaving American Indians like they did with Black Americans. Our country is **diverse** today, yet levels of exploitation based on a person's color of their skin still permeate our American society. I argue fervently the danger of continuing to exploit individuals by saying one's color of their skin makes them different and even subordinate. If we are to eliminate **prejudice,** a belief that one is better in some way, and **discrimination**, actually making a distinction that one is better than another, we need to describe race in a healthy way without the conditioning of social class and skin color. Throughout American history, and even the world, slavery has existed. Unfortunately, in the new millennium there is not a clear sign that it is ending.

In my sociology classes when I teach the myths of race I ask students to roll up their sleeves and put their arm up to the nearby student. Rarely, is there one shade of color that is alike. The evidence is there that if I asked students what is the importance of their particular color of skin I receive responses and questions (Figure 9.1). Race becomes hard to define (as we will see at the end of this chapter in the research on DNA and race done by Dr. Spencer Wells).

FIGURE 9.1 AAP STATEMENT ON RACE

"In the United States both scholars and the general public have been conditioned to viewing human races as natural and separate divisions within the human species based on visible physical differences. With the vast expansion of scientific knowledge in this century, however, it has become clear that human populations are not unambiguous, clearly demarcated, biologically distinct groups. Evidence from the analysis of genetics (e.g., DNA) indicates that most physical variation, about 94%, lies *within* so-called racial groups. Conventional geographic 'racial' groupings differ from one another only in about 6% of their genes. This means that there is greater variation within 'racial' groups than between them. In neighboring populations there is much overlapping of genes and their phenotypic (physical) expressions. Throughout history whenever different groups have come into contact, they have interbred. The continued sharing of genetic materials has maintained all of humankind as a single species."

American Anthropological Association. (1998). Statement on Race. Retrieved from www. aaanet.org/stmts/racepp.htm on September 1, 2012.

We are all part of one species. It is time we address this issue in order for a future of social equality in America and in the world. Just think of the years we have been taught that we are different according to the color of our skin; that a country believed to be based on a democracy was in fact based on hypocrisy. The American Anthropological Association (AAA, 1998) states, "As they were constructing US society, leaders among European-Americans fabricated the cultural/behavioral characteristics associated with each 'race,' linking superior traits with Europeans and negative and inferior ones to blacks and Indians." The social construction of race is real and has permeated American culture. "Ultimately 'race' as an ideology about human differences was subsequently spread to other areas of the world. It became a strategy for dividing, ranking, and controlling colonized people used by colonial powers everywhere" (AAA, 1998).

© Rob Marmion, 2012. Under license from Shutterstock, Inc.

James W. Fox, Jr., assistant professor of law at Stanford University, describes in his article, "Doctrinal Myths and the Management of Cognitive Dissonance: Race, Law, and the Supreme Court's Doctrinal Support of Jim Crow," published in the *Stetson Law Review* (2005, p. 293) that

> [O]ne of the most intriguing questions in the study of American law during the period of Jim Crow is how American society could see itself as the city on a hill for constitutional equality while also creating and enforcing a formidable structure of legally mandated white supremacy ... It is not enough simply to identify the contradiction; we also should look at the mechanisms by which law manages the contradiction to see how equal citizenship principles were so grossly violated, yet so willingly accepted, by the white legal elite ... Through the doctrinal myths of state action, federalism, separate-but-equal, and reasonable segregation, the Court was able to facilitate the white South's re-establishment of legalized white supremacy, which contravened the basic principles of Reconstruction and the Reconstruction Amendments to the Constitution, and yet at the same time argue that it was all along implementing and preserving the equality ideals of those very Amendments.

true equality

What became enacted as law through white dominance still kept Blacks segregated with the help of the law. Now it is time to turn the laws back to **true equality**, policy that does not serve the privileged few but the common people of the United States. Now is time to deconstruct race as inequality and reconstruct race with true equality.

DNA: THE HUMAN GENOME PROJECT

In the past decade results of DNA analysis have opened the "window to the world" for the human species, breaking the ideology of race around the world. The National Geographic Project, headed by the prominent geneticist Dr. Spencer Wells, has transformed our own human history. By a simple swab in the mouth a person can obtain mysteries into the past even up to 10,000 years or more. Wells notes on the National Geographic Genographic website, "the greatest history book ever written is the one hidden in our DNA." Dr. Wells has traveled around the world collecting blood samples from people to find common genetic factors. The research clearly reveals the validity of the statement by the American Anthropological Association (1998) on race (mentioned earlier in this chapter), stating "we are more alike as a human species." According to the National Geographic Genographic project (2012):

> The Genographic Project is seeking to chart new knowledge about the migratory history of the human species by using sophisticated laboratory and computer analysis of DNA contributed by hundreds of thousands of people from around the world. In this unprecedented and of real-time research effort, the Genographic Project is closing the gaps of what science knows today about humankind's ancient migration stories.

As the project moves into the second phase individuals can take a journey to a common beginning thousands of years ago.

ETHNICITY IN MODERN AMERICA

Today in America we are struggling for a modern definition of American **ethnicity**, the culture learned in society. In the sense that ethnicity is learned, what is it that we learn about our culture here in the United States? We learn to get an education, to dream of being rich, to read and write in English (which I prefer to call **Anglish**, a language absorbed from English and newly American culture), and to compete for resources in a society of entrepreneurship and extreme capitalism. The institution of the media, politics, and the economy dominate our ideology system. We value freedom and equality, but exploit the poor, **minorities**— groups of people who are oppressed—women, and children. American culture admires and obsesses over media, celebrity, and the small chance to be rich. Hollywood, Disney, and Universal Studios pride Americans with movies and entertainment. Cell

ethnicity

Anglish

minorities

phones, iPads, and the Internet are part of every American's life, even if they cannot afford to buy media products. We feel shame if we are poor. Americans, however, are hard workers and even overachievers. As we search for the future of American culture, I aspire as a sociologist to focus on true equality.

© Angela Waye, 2012. Under license from Shutterstock, Inc.

CHAPTER NINE *summary*

It is important to view contemporary American culture as a diverse and equal one. American democracy has been marked by white European privilege. People of color in the United States have been exploited and enslaved. DNA and genetics have resolved this issue in an empirical fashion. It is now time to avoid deviation and bring equality to our country for all people. The social construction of race is rearing its shameful head with new possibilities and chances for true democracy and change. We can imagine a country, as the Constitution states, being "equality for all." Someday a great nation may become an even greater nation when we live the values of equality and respect.

Please answer the following discussion questions:

1. What does it mean by the social construction of race in American society? What are the myths of race in American society today? Use the Internet to find specific historical information to support your answers. Please write at least one page with references.

2. Why does the author mention the word *slavery* in modern American society? What are the effects of slavery in America and into the world? Use information to support your ideas.

3. What are steps we can make as Americans to strive toward true equality in our society?

Sociological Key Terms

1. Social construction
2. Slavery
3. Genocide
4. Diversity
5. Prejudice
6. Discrimination
7. True equality
8. Ethnicity
9. Anglish
10. Minorities

CHAPTER *ten*

GERONTOLOGY, THE STUDY OF AGING AND SOCIETY

© Andrey Popov, 2012. Under license from Shutterstock, Inc.

- Defining gerontology and geriatrics
- What are the demographics of aging in America today?
- Explain and define elder abuse and neglect
- Describe the theories of aging?
- List and explain the measures of aging?
- Explain successful aging?
- End-of-life issues and concerns

GERONTOLOGY AND DEMOGRAPHICS

Gerontology is the study of aging and society. Gerontologists want to know how people are aging in our society and what the impact is of the aging population in our communities. **Geriatrics** is the study of medicine for people 65 and older. Geriatricians are medical doctors who prescribe medicine and do routine checks on people 65 and older. **Gerontologists** define the impact of aging populations and identify solutions to help with the increasing population of the elderly. Together both of the fields, gerontology and geriatrics, make major contributions to increasing resources such as living issues, state and county resources, and optimal quality of health.

For the past ten years I have been teaching gerontology to nurses working on bachelor's degrees and to sociology students who are unfamiliar with the dynamics of aging. The health care profession will be impacted by the **baby boomers**, who were born between 1946 and 1964. People are living longer and many are reaching the ages of the **oldest old**, which is 85 and older. A **centenarian** is a person who lives to 100 years old. A **nonagenarian** has lived to 90 years old. An **octogenarian** has lived until 80 years old. People are living longer through new medicines and technology. A **cohort** is a group of people born in the same time period who have experienced significant life events around the same age, such as those born in the 1930s, 1940s, and 1950s.

Gerontologists study the **demographics**, percentages of people growing older in each state and in the country. Knowing the demographics allows for regions of the United States to accommodate the growing senior populations. Note in Chart 10.1 the following statistics from the Administration on Aging specific to the U.S. aging population. As you can see, the demographics of the aging population will impact American society now until 2030 when most baby boomers have reached retirement age. Poverty levels will be dramatic, demanding new programs and resources to minimize the rates of **elder abuse and neglect**, as physical, emotional, and financial exploitation are real concerns for people 65 and older. Women will live on average longer than

geriatrics

gerontologists

baby boomers

oldest old
centenarian
nonagenarian
octogenarian

cohort

demographics

elder abuse and neglect

men, isolating them in their homes and increasing the risk of elder neglect and **depression**. According to the Older American's Act (2010):

> The term "abuse" means the willful—(A) infliction of injury, unreasonable confinement, intimidation, or cruel punishment with resulting physical harm, pain, or mental anguish; or (B) deprivation by a person, including a caregiver, of goods or services that are necessary to avoid physical harm, mental anguish, or mental illness.

Each state may have different variations of the definition of abuse as stated above. The State of Massachusetts has one of the most detailed laws to protect seniors from abuse and neglect. The Massachusetts law specifically mentions emotional abuse:

> Massachusetts law (M.G.L. Chapter 19A) defines elder abuse as an act or omission which results in a serious physical or emotional injury to an elderly person; or is the failure, inability or resistance of an elderly person to provide for himself or herself one or more of the necessities essential for physical and emotional well-being without which the elderly person would be unable to safely remain in the community.

Each state has an **ombudsman program**, which is located in each county area to call and report abuse and neglect in institutions such as **nursing homes (NH), assisted living facilities (ALF)**, and **adult family care homes (AFCH)**. Your call is anonymous, and seriously considered and investigated. If abuse and neglect of a senior is happening in his or her own home, suspicious behavior, especially among family members needs to be reported. Health care workers are obligated to report abuse and neglect immediately.

In 2011, I presented statistics as a gerontologist/sociologist regarding the statistics of elder abuse and neglect in Barnstable County, Massachusetts, at the University of New Hampshire's First Law School National Conference for Violence against Women in Portsmouth, New Hampshire. Barnstable County has one of

depression

*ombudsman
program
nursing homes
(NH)
assisted living
(ALF)
adult family
care homes
(AFCH)*

the highest percentages of people 65 and older in the state of Massachusetts. People 65 and older in this Cape Cod region prize the area beaches, health care, and community support. However, statistics clearly show an increase in the number of any seniors in the area:

> Barnstable County, (Cape Cod): In the year 1990 to 2000 the population of people 60 and older went from 10,508 to 11,953 an increase of **13.8%;** when in 2010 there were 16,028 people 60 and older with an increase of **34.1%** and a projection into 2020 of 23,090 people 60 and older to an increase of **93.2%** consuming the state's average in 2020 of **48.8%.** (The Research Unit, Executive Office of Elder Affairs, based on MISER 12/2002 projections)

According to Elder Affairs of Cape Cod in 2011:

> Elders must be 60+ years of age and live "in the community." Elders who reside as long term residents in nursing facilities would not be within our jurisdiction. Additionally, in terms of protective services, there needs to be an "ongoing and personal relationship" between the Elder and the alleged perpetrator. For example, if an elder was assaulted and/or exploited by a stranger, we would refer the case directly to the police, DA, etc.

As you can see on Cape Cod, a person 60 and older and who lives in the community eligible for county services; however, those in an institution are protected by the state ombudsman program. Under the Older Americans Act seniors have access to aging services in each county of the United States. If you do an Internet search for the county you live in (e.g., Barnstable County + Aging Services) you will find the **Area Agency on Aging (AAA).** If you worry about a senior friend or family member in another state you can call the local county AAA, then let the senior know that you are sending someone to assess their situation and eligibility for services. The AAA can help increase the quality of life for people 65 and older and supply resources to minimize elder abuse and neglect.

CHART 10.1 A PROFILE OF OLDER AMERICANS, 2011

Highlights*
- The older population (65+) numbered 40.4 million in 2010, an increase of 5.4 million or 15.3% since 2000.
- The number of Americans aged 45–64, who will reach 65 over the next two decades, increased by 31% during this decade.
- Over one in every eight, or 13.1%, of the population is an older American.
- Persons reaching age 65 have an average life expectancy of an additional 18.8 years (20.0 years for females and 17.3 years for males).
- Older women outnumber older men at 23 million older women to 17.5 million older men.
- In 2010, 20.0% of persons 65+ were minorities—8.4% were African-Americans.** Persons of Hispanic origin (who may be of any race) represented 6.9% of the older population. About 3.5% were Asian or Pacific Islander,** and less than 1% were American Indian or Native Alaskan.** In addition, 0.8% of persons 65+ identified themselves as being of two or more races.
- Older men were much more likely to be married than older women—72% of men vs. 42% of women (Figure 2). 40% of older women in 2010 were widows.
- About 29% (11.3 million) of noninstitutionalized older persons live alone (8.1 million women, 3.2 million men).
- Almost half of older women (47%) age 75+ live alone.
- About 485,000 grandparents aged 65 or more had the primary responsibility for their grandchildren who lived with them.
- The population 65 and over has increased from 35 million in 2000 to 40 million in 2010 (a 15% increase) and is projected to increase to 55 million in 2020 (a 36% increase for that decade).
- The 85+ population is projected to increase from 5.5 million in 2010 to 6.6 million in 2020 (19%) for that decade.
- Minority populations have increased from 5.7 million in 2000 (16.3% of the elderly population) to 8.1 million in 2010 (20% of the elderly) and are projected to increase to 13.1 million in 2020 (24% of the elderly).
- The median income of older persons in 2010 was $25,704 for males and $15,072 for females. Median money income (after adjusting for inflation) of all households headed by older people fell 1.5% (not statistically significant) from 2009 to 2010. Households containing

families headed by persons 65+ reported a median income in 2010 of $45,763.

- The major sources of income as reported by older persons in 2009 were Social Security (reported by 87% of older persons), income from assets (reported by 53%), private pensions (reported by 28%), government employee pensions (reported by 14%), and earnings (reported by 26%).
- Social Security constituted 90% or more of the income received by 35% of beneficiaries in 2009 (22% of married couples and 43% of non-married beneficiaries).
- Almost 3.5 million elderly persons (9.0%) were below the poverty level in 2010. This poverty rate is not statistically different from the poverty rate in 2009 (8.9%). During 2011, the U.S. Census Bureau also released a new Supplemental Poverty Measure (SPM) which takes into account regional variations in the livings costs, non-cash benefits received, and non-discretionary expenditures but does not replace the official poverty measure. The SPM shows a poverty level for older persons of 15.9%, an increase of over 75% over the official rate of 9.0% mainly due to medical out-of-pocket expenses.
- About 11% (3.7 million) of older Medicare enrollees received personal care from a paid or unpaid source in 1999.

*Principal sources of data for the Profile are the U.S. Census Bureau, the National Center for Health Statistics, and the Bureau of Labor Statistics. The Profile incorporates the latest data available but not all items are updated on an annual basis.

MEASURES AND THEORIES OF AGING

Gerontologists use four measures in determining the aging process:

1. Chronological—number of years one has aged (e.g., Sheila is 76 years old.).
2. Biological—genetic and physical markers of aging (e.g., David's eyesight at the age of 40 required glasses for reading.).
3. Social—interaction with others (e.g., staying in contact with family, friends, and the community).
4. Psychological—mental health and well-being (Janet feels like she is 25 years old despite her age of 65.).

Gerontologists use three theories to explain successful aging:

1. Activity theory—remaining physically and mentally active throughout the senior years (e.g., Sue has retired but remains very active with her community.).
2. Continuity theory—stable personality traits and routines over the years (e.g., John has retired yet still runs five miles every morning.).
3. Disengagement theory—withdrawing from society after retirement (e.g., Mary has retired, but seldom interacts with her friends, family, and community.).

Activity theory and continuity theory show successful aging. Disengagement theory is a concern for friends, family, and community. When you see a senior isolated, this person is at risk for self-neglect and social isolation which can lead to depression, which is treatable but ultimately can increase odds for suicide. **Successful aging** reflects on good mental and social health, despite physical limitations and chronic disease.

successful aging

END-OF-LIFE ISSUES

Depression is a real concern for the U.S. senior population due to loss of loved ones, physical illness, and hormonal imbalances. Depression is treatable. Geriatricians recommend treating depression with medicine for seniors who are experiencing clinical depression of more than six months. By treating depression along with physical illness, the quality of life increases. Quality of life is the key to successful aging. If depression is not treated or managed, then the quality of life will decrease as seen in self-neglect of people 65 and older. Symptoms of **dementia**, or the loss of memory, may or may not be depression or overuse of medication. In order to diagnose dementia, the illness of depression or **delirium** (a temporary loss of memory and brain function) needs to be ruled out along with any physical causes contributing to the symptoms. **Alzheimer's disease**, complete loss of memory, can be empirically diagnosed after death (postmortem) by observing tangles and plaques in the brain.

The prominent gerontologist David Snowden (2001) did a study on Alzheimer's disease using the Sisters of Notre Dame, a group of religious nuns. The nuns agreed to donate their brains after death. You can read about this study in the book, *Aging with Grace*. Snowden (2001) "analyzes the nun's early childhood writings and biographies and compares to see if language played a role in reducing the chances of having symptoms of Alzheimer's disease." Snowden (2001) "also notes the uniqueness of a nun convent and community in which similar patterns of behavior such as teaching and life-long learning contributed to the health of the nuns' brains." Snowden continues to note "positive prayer and social support contributed in this target population to more years of health brain activity." The results of Snowden's study is limited to just the nun population, but allows us to ask more questions to further the research on this devastating disease.

End-of-life issues include the right to die and the right to make one's own choices. Legal issues are important at the end of life. Hiring an elder attorney to help with maintaining one's independence and to stay in the home for the longest time is critical for many seniors. Seniors tend not to ask for help and have made life decisions for their final days. Saving money for retirement is also critical. People 65 and older transition better into retirement when money is not a factor. The reality is many seniors, especially women, will live in poverty. I just recently heard seniors are increasingly stealing from local drug stores and retail stores to get essentials such as aspirin and denture cream. Society needs to do more to help seniors to maintain aging in place, and create optimal quality of life. **Living wills** provide one's final wishes when death is near. For example, a person may designate not to have oxygen anymore so that the final days come sooner. With a living will this wish can be carried out.

CHAPTER TEN *summary*

We have merely skimmed the surface in this chapter regarding the topic of aging and society. You can take an upper-level sociology class to learn more about this topic, including information on Medicare and Medicaid. Aging successfully can be measured on a chronological, biological, social, or psychological basis. Theories of aging include activity, continuity, and disengagement theory. Area Agencies on Aging are mandated by the federal Older Americans Act to help seniors with important resources such as nursing, food, and shelter. Important statistics from the Administration on Aging clearly reflect the needs for American society to prepare for the baby boomers aging in the next twenty years. Depression, dementia, and Alzheimer's disease are real concerns for people 65 and older. The economics of aging include preparing financially to live a better quality of life. What we do not invest for our seniors now will cost society more in the long term. However, the morality of helping our older population starts with gerontologists and geriatricians working together; and you report signs of elder abuse and neglect in your own community. Legal issues are important when facing death in the final years. Final wishes can be legal in a living will and finances and estates can be managed by elder lawyers. Successful aging can be achieved and passed down for the younger generation to learn and live by.

Please answer the following discussion questions:

1. Define gerontology and geriatrics. What are the differences between the two fields? What are the similarities? Please write two paragraphs with specific examples.
2. Choose two of the statistics provided in Chart 10.1. What is your opinion about each statistic and why? How does each statistic impact our society even your own community?

3. Research the Area Agency on Aging in your county. List ten programs and the services provided by each program. Also research your state's Department of Elder Affairs. List five programs and the services provided by the state program. In one paragraph write a reflection on what you have found.

Sociological Key Terms

1. Gerontology
2. Geriatrics
3. Gerontologists
4. Baby boomer
5. Oldest old
6. Centarian
7. Nonagenarian
8. Octogenarian
9. Cohort
10. Demographics
11. Elder abuse and neglect
12. Depression
13. Ombudsman program
14. Nursing home (NH)
15. Assisted living facility (ALF)
16. Adult family care home (AFCH)
17. Area Agency on Aging (AAA)
18. Successful aging
19. Dementia
20. Delirium
21. Alzheimer's disease
22. Living will

REFERENCES

Administration on Aging. (2012). www.aoa.gov

American Anthropological Association. (1998). *Statement on Race.* Retrieved September 1, 2012, from www.aaanet.org/stmts/racepp.htm

Bachman, R., Zaykowski, H., Lanier, C., Poteyeva, M., & Kallmyer, R. (2010). Estimating the Magnitude of Rape and Sexual Assault Against American Indian and Alaska Native (AIAN) Women. *Australian & New Zealand Journal of Criminology (Australian Academic Press), 43*(2), 199–222. doi:10.1375/acri.43.2.199

Barnstable County, Massachusetts Statistics. (2002). Population Growth into 2020. The Research Unit, Executive Office of Elder Affairs, based on MISER 12/2002 projections.

Barry, K. (1981). The Underground Economic System of Pimping. *Journal of International Affairs, 35*(1), 117.

Bernard, B. (1997). Turning It Around for All Youth: From Risk to Resilience. *ERIC Clearinghouse on Urban Education, 126.*

Canfield, A. (2007). Stephen King's Dolores Claiborne and Rose Madder: A Literary Backlash Against Domestic Violence. *Journal of American Culture, (30)*4, 391–401.

Centers for Disease Control and Prevention (CDC). (2012). www.cdc.gov

Comte, A. (1957). *A General View of Positivism: Centenary Edition.* New York: Speller & Sons.

Cooley, C.H. (2012). *Charles Horton Cooley*. Retrieved from www.bolenderinitiatives.com/sociology/charles-horton-cooley-1864-1929

DuBois, W.E. (1968). *A Soliloquy on Viewing My Life from the Last Decade of Its First Century*.

Edwards, E.E. (1934). American Indian Contributions to American History. *Minnesota History, 15*(3).

Fox Jr., J.W. (2005). Doctrinal Myths and the Myths of Management of Cognitive Dissonance: Race, Law, and the Supreme Courts Doctrinal Support of Jim Crow. *34, 293–242.*

Froggio, G. (2007). Strain and Juvenile Delinquency: A Critical Review of Agnew's General Strain Theory. *Journal of Loss & Trauma, 12*(4), 383–418.

Giddens, A. (Ed.). (1986). *Durkheim on Politics and the State*. Stanford, CT: Stanford University Press.

Godin, B. (2010). Innovation Without the Word: William F. Ogburn's Contribution to the Study of Technological Innovation. *Minerva, 48,* 277–307.

Jacobs, G. (2006). *Charles Horton Cooley: Imagining Social Reality*. Amherst: University of Massachusetts Press.

Janice, I.L. (1972). *Victims of Groupthink*. Boston: Houghton Mifflin Company.

Kirk, D. (2009). Consenting Adults. *Journal of Criminal Law, 73*(4), 281–283.

Koll, S. (2009). Is Bureaucracy Compatible with Democracy? *South African Journal of Philosophy, 28*(2), 134–145.

Kozol, J. (1988). Why Are the Homeless Crazy? *Harper's*

Kozol, J. (1992). *Savage Inequalities*. New York: HarperCollins.

Martineau, H. (1837: 1966). *Society in America*. London: Saunders and Oatley; New York: AM Press.

Martin, M. (2000). *Verstehen: The Uses of Understanding in Social Sciences*. New Brunswick, NJ: Transaction Publishers.

Marx, K., and Eastman, Max (Ed.). (1932). *Capital and Other Writings by Karl Marx*. New York: The Modern Library.

McClure, C. (2011) *Attitudes on Care Giving and Aging*. West Barnstable, MA: Cape Cod Community College.

Mills, C.W. (1954). The Structure of Power in American Society. *British Journal of Sociology, 9*(1), 29–41.

Minke, L. (2011). The Effects of Mixing Offenders with Non-Offenders: Findings from Danish Quasi-Experiment. *Journal of Scandinavian Studies in Criminology & Crime Prevention, 12*(1), 80–99. doi:10.1080/14043858.2011.561624

Murphy, E. (2011). *Cape Cod and the Islands Statistics on Elder Abuse and Neglect.* Cape Cod, MA: Adult Protective Services.

Nakhaie, M., Silverman, R.A., & LaGrange, T.C. (2000). Self-Control and Social Control: An Examination of Gender, Ethnicity, Class and Delinquency. *Canadian Journal of Sociology, 25*(1), 35–59.

National Crime Victimization Survey. (2012). Indicators of School Crime Safety. Retrieved February 2012, from http://bjs.ojp.usdoj.gov/content/pub/pdf/iscs11.pdf

National Opinion Research Center. (2012). Retrieved from www3.norc.org/GSS+Website/About+GSS/About+NORC/

Non-profit Organizations. (2007). In *Palgrave Macmillan Dictionary of Political Thought.* Retrieved from www.credoreference.com/entry/macpt/non_profit_organizations

Öun, I. (2012). Work-Family Conflict in the Nordic Countries: A Comparative Analysis. *Journal of Comparative Family Studies, 43*(2), 165–184.

Owens, R.G., & Valesky, T.C. (2011). *Organizational Behavior in Education: Leadership and School Reform* (10th ed.). Boston: Pearson, Inc.

Policar, H. (2010). The Shadow of the American Dream: The Clash of Class Ascension and Shame. *Revision, 31*(1), 19–31.

Roden, & Stewart. (2012). Resilience in Elderly Survivors of Child Maltreatment. *Child Abuse and Neglect, 33*, 139-147.

Rutter, M. (2012). Presentation on Developmental Psychology.

Schulz, S. (2004). Problems with the Versatility Construct of Gottfredson and Hirschi's General Theory of Crime. *European Journal of Crime, Criminal Law & Criminal Justice, 12*(1), 61–82.

Snow, R.C. (2007). Sex, Gender, and Vulnerability. *Population Studies Center Research Report 07-628.* Ann Arbor: University of Michigan School of Public Health.

Snowden, D. (2001). *Aging with Grace.* New York: Bantam Books.

Straus, M.A. (2008). Bucking the Tide in Family Violence. *Trauma, Violence, and Abuse, 9*(4), 191–213.

U.S. Census. (2012, July). Retrieved from www.census.gov

Wells, S. (2012). *The Genome Project.* Washington, DC: The National Geographic Society.

Witherspoon, B. (2012). School Wide Approaches for Fostering Resiliency.

World Health Organization. (2012). www.who.org